THE DAY MY FATHER DIED

Women Share Their Stories
of Love, Loss, and Life

EDITED BY DIANA AJJAN

RUNNING PRESS
Philadelphia, Pennsylvania

Canadian representatives: General Publishing Co., Ltd., 30 Lesmill Road, Don Mills, Ontario M3B 2T6. International representatives: Worldwide Media Services, Inc., 30 Montgomery Street, Jersey City, New Jersey 07302.

9 8 7 6 5 4 3 2 1
Digit on the right indicates the number of this printing.

Library of Congress Cataloging-in-Publication Number 93–85509

ISBN 1–56138–189–6

The editor and publisher gratefully acknowledge the permission of the following to reproduce copyrighted material in this book; Pp. 23, 33, 35: "Keeping Quiet," "Love at First Sight I," and "Love at First Sight II" by Morgan Henderson copyright © 1993 by Morgan Henderson; p. 55: "Father's Chair Will Be Empty" by Melissa Dribben, reprinted with permission of *The Record* of Hackensack, NJ; p. 59: Excerpted from *Sweet Summer: Growing Up With and Without My Dad* by Bebe Moore Campbell, copyright © 1989 by Bebe Moore Campbell, reprinted by permission of G.P. Putnam's Sons, all rights reserved; p. 133: Excerpted from *Sophia: Living and Loving* by Sophia Loren with A. E. Hotchner, reprinted with permission of William Morrow; p. 139: Excerpted from *The Bookmaker's Daughter* by Shirley Abbott, copyright © 1991 by Shirley Abbott, reprinted by permission of Ticknor & Fields/Houghton Mifflin Co., all rights reserved; p. 191: "My Father's Death," copyright © 1978, 1994 by Marcia Lee Falk. Excerpted from *The Book of Blessings: A Feminist-Jewish Reconstruction of Prayer* by Marcia Falk, forthcoming, 1995, from HarperSan Francisco. Used by permission of the author; p. 193: "Dad's Dying" by Candyce H. Stapen from *Storms and Rainbows*, copyright © 1991 by Candyce H. Stapen, reprinted by permission of the author.

The publisher would like to acknowledge the help of Parke Bowman and Jill Feldman during the compilation of this book.

Cover design by E. June Roberts
Front cover photograph by Jessica Helfand
Back cover and flap photographs provided by Amy Biancolli and Candyce H. Stapen
Interior design by Nancy Loggins
Edited by Melissa Stein
Typography: Adobe Garamond by Deborah Lugar
Printed in Hong Kong

This book may be ordered by mail from the publisher.
Please add $2.50 for postage and handling.
But try your bookstore first!

Running Press Book Publishers
125 South Twenty-second Street
Philadelphia, Pennsylvania 19103–4399

CONTENTS

The publishers and the editor would like to thank all of the writers for their courage, commitment, and generosity in contributing to this anthology.

INTRODUCTION

THE DAY MY FATHER DIED brings together a diverse and courageous group of women who write eloquently of the bond shared only by daughters and fathers. Although their experiences vary greatly, each writer attests to the power of her father—the first important man in her life—to profoundly influence her growth as an individual. Just as each relationship portrayed here is unique, so are the ways in which each woman deals with the loss of her father, revealing the extraordinary strength and resources she may find to help her overcome grief.

The twenty-five writers included in this anthology candidly relate how they have come to terms with their fathers' deaths. Some, like Antoinette Bosco and Gloria Averbuch, warmly remember loving and generous fathers, and mourn the passing of these great inspirations in their lives. Others grieve over lost opportunities to rekindle—or even begin—relationships with their fathers.

Each of these writers finds herself faced with the challenge of reliving her relationship with her father in order to move forward in her life. In "Archaeology," Joan Allison Shiel embarks on a journey of her own as she sifts through her father's journals and collections, attempting to discover a man she never knew. Journalist Kim Rich, in "Johnny's Girl," recounts the story of her father's murder when she was only fifteen years old, and tells how she later pieced together the fragments of her father's life in order to better understand her own. In "The Man in the Picture," Amy Biancolli struggles to recall her father as he was before being stricken by Alzheimer's Disease, and she reclaims him through childhood memories.

Among the courageous women who speak out in this anthology are those who have had to come to terms with the sins of their fathers. Substance abuse, excessive gambling, and sexual abuse have confounded many of these relationships and caused lasting emotional scars. In "Journey," Andrea Chapin tries to reconcile conflicting truths: her father was clearly an outstanding man, but he was also an alcoholic. Dolores Schwartz, in her stirring essay "The Deaths of the Fathers," proclaims that she may never be at peace with her father, because she cannot erase, rationalize, or accept the damaging effects of sexual abuse. And how can a daughter possibly understand why her father would abandon her by taking his own life? Dea Mallin reflects with wisdom on her experience of coping with her father's suicide.

Many of these women, kept at an emotional distance from their fathers for varied and complex reasons, were prevented from knowing them in life. Some of these writers found that a greater understanding of their fathers, as parents and as people, healed old wounds and softened the pain of loss.

The death of someone we love suddenly highlights our own mortality. The experience can bring with it a hidden blessing: the realization that people are precious in one's life, and one should always make the effort to know them. It is in this understanding that many women find their comfort, and make their uneasy—but vital—peace with death.

As many of these writers illustrate, light and hope often emanate from otherwise mournful events. Sophia Loren found that despite a troubled relationship with her father, his death compelled her to reach out to the brother she never really knew. Similarly, in Janet Burroway's "Dad Scattered" and Constance Schraft's "This is George," we watch family members draw together, gaining strength and reasserting the bonds of the living.

Through a rediscovered photograph, a recollection of childhood, or the remembered echo of a beloved voice, these women reveal how they keep their fathers alive. "I think that the phoenix that rises from the ashes is feathered in love," Dea Mallin writes, "and that love takes wing and alights on those in need."

For these women, their fathers' spirits and legacies live on in relationships that continually change and grow, through shared memories and new-found wisdom.

Out of Time

Karen Stabiner

WHEN I WAS BORN my father bought me a set of dishes. I am not talking about department-store baby dishes embossed with nursery rhymes and characters. My father was in restaurant supply—the Ira in the Ira China Company, started by his father in the 1920s, soon after my father's birth. So he ordered heavy white restaurant china decorated with a mauve border that enclosed the words "Karen Sue." There were two small cups, one mug, two fruit dishes, two salad plates and two lunch plates. I guess he assumed that everyone would be as glad to see me as he was, that I would never take a solitary meal.

I grew into, and out of, the dishes. Thirty-seven years later I still have them, and a morning espresso fits very nicely into one of the cups.

He had nine months to prepare for my arrival, but when I showed up words failed him. He was prepared, but he wasn't ready. He couldn't be ready. This had never happened to him before.

Last month he died of lung cancer. Like him, I had about nine months to prepare for what was coming. Like him, I was not ready. This had never happened to me before.

My father turned 65 four months before he died—too young, as countless people sought to remind me when I was in Chicago for the funeral. They meant it as consolation, though I think they said it, in part, to keep fear at bay. If he was too young to die, if they could convince themselves that he was an exception, then they, his peers, were not yet in jeopardy. People also told me that I was too young to lose a parent—as if his death weren't sadness enough, as if I needed to feel cheated to achieve despair.

Then, a week after his death, *The New York Times* officially declared his departure premature. According to an article in the *Times*, we were an actuarial anomaly: Most adults reach their 40s or 50s before they have to face dealing with an infirm or elderly parent. For a moment I was happy being indignant. This was a fluke, a cosmic computer glitch. Clearly they were supposed to take the next dad in the alphabet who was probably 84, and not my father. We could straighten this out and get him back—it was merely a matter of finding the appropriate office and filling out the necessary forms.

But the pain of his death has nothing to do with anyone's age, really; it has to do with running out of time. My father never talked about living to the ripe old age of 71, but he had talked, incessantly, about wanting to reach his 50th wedding anniversary and stick his kids for a big party.

When he first learned he was ill he mentioned that party more often, along with other upcoming events that he planned to attend. He told his doctors of his intentions as if they were proof that he was not meant to die now, as if looking forward to happiness were a symptom of health. For a short time he tried to believe, and convince the rest of us, that a full calendar could fight disease.

But he was smart enough to comprehend the odds, which were dreadful, and the results of the chemotherapy and radiation, which were nil. He quickly came to see that he was dying. He began to act differently.

As his illness progressed he started calling almost daily, never for any specific reason, but just to hear what the events of a particular Tuesday, or Sunday morning, had been. He knew, though he wouldn't admit it, that there would soon be days without him, mundane details that he would miss. We knew it too—and that knowledge made us all a little crazy. We had always had the luxury of endless time, time enough to ignore each other once in a while, and now we had a deadline. I eagerly recited the events of my day for him, as if very full days, now, could make up for empty ones later.

In Chicago, after he died, my sister and I wandered around my parents' house and confessed to the same disoriented, eerie sensation—that my father would, at any moment, walk into the room. It was our hearts' wish; we were greedy to see him again.

For his death didn't age us—it cut us loose. There was no future with him anymore. All the talk of how young we were was a useless entreaty, a digging in of our heels: Please, not yet.

The fact is, my dad's death makes me middle aged, in a way that has nothing to do with chronology, lifestyle, or state of mind. Anyone who is old enough to have babies and lose a parent is middle-aged, no matter what the birth certificate says. I used to know that death was inevitable like I knew that a billion people lived in China: I had the information and was incapable of comprehending it. Now I have watched my father lose his life. I can see the end in both directions— there is no father between me and death. I am formally, finitely, in the middle.

For years he was responsible for me—he bought me kilts and matching knee socks, punched the driver of a car who skidded into us on the way to my piano lesson one Saturday, taught me to eat oysters, deflated my academic pretensions with infuriating lectures about surviving in the real world, and strong-armed everyone he knew into buying my books. He sang songs to me and sent me restaurant equipment.

Ever the salesman, he promoted the illusion of perpetual motion. We were always doing something; we never much thought about not. When he got very sick he apologized, often, for screwing up. Once he asked me, "What have I done to you?" I think he was sorry that he couldn't spare us seeing death, that in his absence there would always be a little window right onto it.

A week before he died I flew to Chicago, not because he was in any shape to talk to me, but because my mother was exhausted. I spent most of the time with her. One morning we heard a voice from upstairs: "Isn't anybody else up around this house?" I ran upstairs and he looked at the cup in my hand. "Whatcha got there?" he asked.

"Coffee."

"Sit down here. Can I join you?"

He hadn't wanted coffee for weeks—some side effect of the chemotherapy. Still, he had always believed in dining as a social expression of affection. He wasn't really interested in the coffee; when the nurse brought it up he took two sips. But we had our coffee together.

That was the last time I spoke with him. I left that afternoon, and the next time I returned was for his funeral. Now I am responsible for him, as is anyone who cared for him. What life he has is up to us, in our hearts, in the stories we recall.

I do not feel old, but I do feel weary. My mind ransacks history looking for solace, remembering things I haven't thought about in years. In any given day, I am all the ages I ever was with him. I am a writer working on a book, making appointments, meeting deadlines—and I am a 13-year-old in a green vinyl jacket slogging along a Colorado resort trail with my dad, both of us trying to kick some life into our barnsour horses.

I am the eldest daughter of a dead man, and I am daddy's little girl; I am at an age, startlingly, when a memory is as sweet as a dream.

June 24, 1952

Nancy Baker Rullo

I HATED THE END of school. Especially this year. Fifth grade was the best and I had the top average in the class again. I had only one real rival, Sigrid Neuman, and since she was the star in all the school plays, wore a bra, and had a thirteen-year-old boyfriend, I had to beat her out in grades. Being her best friend wasn't easy.

Our class had Sister Mary Daniel for the third time. She was the only nun who never pulled me aside to ask if I was praying for my "poor father" and helping my "poor mother" take care of the younger children. No class ever had the same teacher more than once but we were her class—she said so—and she was our teacher. In spring and in the autumn we listened faithfully to the Brooklyn Dodgers. The small black radio was on the window sill, hopefully far from the omniscient eyes and ears of The Mighty Midget, Sister Mary Ancilla, the principal of Saint Patrick's School.

We couldn't cheer or shout, but when Duke Snider was at bat we found ourselves out of our seats and clustered around Sister Mary

Daniel's desk. She never seemed to notice as the girls clutched her hands, twirling the simple gold band around her wedding ring finger, traced the heavy black wooden rosary beads suspended from her broad belt, and wound themselves in the sheer black veil. The boys absently played with the objects on her desk, muttering phrases learned from their Little League games. If the inning got very tense she whispered "Hail Mary . . ." and we tagged quietly along, just loud enough to be noticed by God, and not by Sister Mary Ancilla. I was good at prayer. A whole rosary rarely took me longer than six minutes. But I was just beginning to realize that true prayer was a grander conception, a greater spiritual depth that I had yet to enter. I prayed anyway. A hit or, please God, a home run, could stop our prayer dead and replace it with muffled shrieks and kisses on her hands, face, rosary, and crucifix.

Fifth grade was over, we knew we'd never have Sister Mary Daniel again, and in five days I would leave with Sigrid for Camp Immaculata. I had never been away to camp. I never knew anyone who had. It was a treat planned by relatives to stop my worrying about what might be happening at home. I hadn't been home since Easter Sunday when I was bundled off to live with our friends, Marge and George Clark. They lived on the block between my house and Saint Patrick's School and Marge was the most glamorous woman in the neighborhood. She wore caftans and pink mules around the house, served swordfish and prime rib, and let me stay home from school if I complained of a sore throat. On those glorious spring days we lay on hammocks in her back yard, in our underwear, reading magazines. Once I saw her necking with George on the living room couch. Marge was not a Catholic.

I loved Marge and now I had only myself to blame that I no longer lived in her house. Instead I lived up at "The Mansion" with my Aunt Mary Ann, Uncle Andy, five little cousins and a long line of maids with interchangeable faces. One day, walking alone from school to Marge's house, I had decided to go home, to my own home, the house where I had lived from the day I was born. If I stood in the middle of the street in front of Marge's house I was able to see it. No one ever said I couldn't go home, but for two months I hadn't. I hadn't walked that extra block. I hadn't seen my mother, or my father, whose long sickness caused this disruption in my life. So that day I kept on walking, down the block, across Union Street, up the sidewalk and through the front door. I didn't think to knock.

Stepping into the tiny living room, I instantly sensed the shock that my ten-year-old presence, bookbag in arms, had caused. I stood firmly on the only right I knew. This was my house. All the nurses, aunts, neighbors, and friends who gathered there daily had other places to retreat to, but this was mine. I smiled at them, but my voice shook as I announced my intention of visiting for the afternoon. My mother was nowhere in sight. I dropped the bookbag at my feet and walked past the arms held out for hugs and the faces with nervous smiles. I walked quickly into the bedroom that had always been mine.

The white room shimmered in late afternoon light and my father lay on a hospital bed in the center of it. Next to him was a table with a glass of water and the thick brown crucifix that unmistakenly held the Sacrament of Extreme Unction. I kept trying to look at my father—the clam digger, the musician, the boat builder—but it was impossible. His eyes finally opened and I saw him smile at me, but I couldn't look at the thin, hollow face in that tall, white bed. I stubbornly fixed my eyes on the cross in a question that didn't need an answer.

"Father Purick brought it to me," he said quietly. "And sometimes if I'm very sick they anoint me and I feel much better."

I nodded silently. Looking down at my saddle shoes, I told him about winning a spelling bee in school. That was a lie. I had spelled "tongue" wrong. But he was always so proud that I was smart. I stood in the echoing room until Sister Mary Daniel, who had been called from the convent, came bustling in to escort me to Marge's.

Two days later I received an invitation to live at "The Mansion," and my mother phoned to let me know how hurt they would be if I didn't accept. Never one to hurt peoples' feelings, I moved.

I was alone in that huge house. My younger cousins had friends who lived nearby. Uncle Andy left early for the city, and I never knew where my aunt was. She didn't stay home with me like Marge did. I was afraid of the maids. After school I wandered the grounds and found secret hiding places in rows of hedges and flowering bushes. And now that school was out the worst was about to happen.

Sigrid had told me what camp would be like. She was an expert on everything, even camp, although she had never been there. We would be together in the bunks and in all of our activities, she said, except swimming of course, since she was a good swimmer and I was still afraid to put my head under water. It was true. Years of lessons had not cured me, and although I managed to get by with the dog paddle and a modified side stroke, camp would be humiliating. I would stay in the shallow water with the babies and Sigrid would go diving off the raft with the other ten-year-olds. The special intention in my nightly prayer was divided between the routine plea for my father's renewed health and a miracle cure for hydrophobia.

The day after school ended I woke early and hid outdoors under a clutch of evergreen bushes chosen for their exquisite privacy and good view of the yard. I practiced cupping my hands, moving my arms in Australian crawl motions and bobbing my head up and down in imaginary water. I was surprised no one called me in for breakfast. I saw my aunt jump into her station wagon and race down the driveway. I worked harder on my strokes. Maybe she thought I had run away and was going to call in the police. But I was not going to suffer humiliation in camp so I stayed, breathing in and out until I was so hot I lay down in the cool sandy soil and rested my head in my arms. I may have fallen asleep. Suddenly I heard my name being called from the back porch in the unmistakable Caribbean lilt of the newest maid.

"Nancy, your oncle ees cahming. You are going to see your mahther. Cahm quickly!"

I exploded from the bushes, scraping my dirty face on a branch, and ran to the house to clean up. But the maid sent me back outside saying I should wait in the front yard. The black Buick rolled in as I reached the end of the driveway and my Uncle Ed, the priest, let me in the front seat. We loved him the best of all the uncles. He always had treats in his shiny black pockets, and if he came to visit at night he would roar into the bedroom, roll us up in blankets and toss us in the air.

As soon as I slid into the car today, though, I could sense that he was different. He always mumbled a little when he talked and I couldn't seem to hear what he was saying. My mind stopped working in the middle of his first sentence. Shredded cardboard filled my brain but words like "brave," "Heaven," and "prayers" poked through. I felt myself slumping against my uncle as if my skeleton had dissolved. We didn't drive toward my house as I expected. We pulled onto my grandfather's street. This was where our large Irish family gathered on the most formal occasions. Bitter tastes filled my mouth and I licked the dirty tears that started down my cheeks. I hadn't heard a recognizable sentence but I knew what he was trying to say. I knew and I hated it.

"Is Daddy dead?"

I felt so dumb, so thick, so helplessly stupid. He parked the car in the driveway but I couldn't imagine what I was expected to do next.

Uncle Ed put his arms around me and he choked as he tried to answer my question. With horror I noticed his own tears. I screamed at him, fighting his arms away.

"No, no, no. I want my mother. No, no, he's not. I prayed. I did. I want my mother!"

The blackness of the Buick's interior was wrapped around me as I stumbled past the rhododendron and salvia lining the path to the house. The French doors opened from a stone patio into the living room and quiet voices came through, but my vision was limited to my mother's face. She sat alone in that crowded room, on a large sofa. She was all I needed and her eyes were on mine. I buried myself in her dress with my skinny legs tangled in the legs of the coffee table. My head and chest ached from the fear and grief that were trying to find an explanation or a denial. Familiar voices spoke to me from the borders of the room:

"Don't cry."

"You'll upset your mother."

"Sit up. Sit up on the couch."

"You're a big girl."

"Don't cry."

"Your mother needs you to be a big girl."

"Be good. Don't cry."

I sat up on the couch, my mother's arms around me. We didn't speak. Maybe she couldn't. The late June sunlight hammered off the white walls. I saw my dirty knees and covered them with my hands, but my hands were shamefully grimy, too. The distant faces, usually all so comfortable, had a harsh, cold, drawn look. I glanced around quickly looking for a smile, anywhere, from anyone. We sat there for a long time. I tried not to cry. My whole life had just changed. I was never going to be good enough, or smart enough, to prevent disaster from striking. I hadn't prayed enough. I hadn't really prayed at all.

I went back to "The Mansion" in the Buick. The house seemed

empty but I could hear maids and cooks talking in the kitchen. I walked through the empty library and even took a few steps into the formal living room which was off-limits to children. The playroom was deserted, and the toys weren't mine, anyway. In my bedroom I stood looking out the window. My brain was hollow, but my world was in chaos. How could I not have known? A maid came in to tell me I had a telephone call. It was Sigrid.

"Hello," she said in a new, formal voice. "My mom told me that your father died and I wanted to say I'm sorry. Do you feel like coming over today?"

So this was what I was in for. Her boldness in everything extended to the unimaginable. It had not occurred to me yet that my private horror and shame was also public. It was going to be the talk of the town. My friends knew, the nuns knew, they probably even knew at Camp Immaculata. I stared at the brown, gleaming surface of the sideboard that held the black phone.

"No, thanks." I tried to sound normal, even casual. "I'm real busy today. I'm studying algebra this summer. But tomorrow maybe we can go to the beach. I need to learn to swim before camp."

Sigrid was quiet for a long time. I heard her put her hand over the mouthpiece and talk to her mother.

"Okay. Tomorrow I'll help you learn to swim. We'll swim out to the raft together at camp. Okay?"

I rushed out into the mid-afternoon heat to get to the library before Sigrid did. I took out the easiest book on algebra I could find. Carrying my new treasure into the house I called to the maid for a glass of lemonade to be delivered to the forbidden living room. The rest of the day was spent studying the mystery of numbers represented by x. It was a mystery I had hopes of conquering without the intercession of prayers. No one dared disturb me.

KEEPING QUIET
MORGAN HENDERSON

IT'S FUNNY, HOW YOU remember and disremember at the same time. I get impressions, speed-of-light pictures that flash by like subliminal advertising, or one of those tiny thumb-books where you flip through pages of stick drawings and see a jerky cartoon. If I try to freeze-frame one picture, it disappears, a Polaroid photo going backwards from color to blank.

When my father died at age 55, I went home to Massachusetts for the funeral. My Uncle Roy, my father's brother, paced our living room, saying, "*I didn't know, I didn't know he was that sick.*"

None of us knew, really. We didn't want to know. We didn't know what to do, how to stop it, what to say to him. Now, sitting in the living room the day of his funeral, we still don't know how to talk to each other. We're usually teetotalers, but this afternoon my mother, my brothers and sister, my aunts and uncles pour themselves cups of vodka and orange juice from the cut glass punch bowl. People tell family stories, to loud hysteric laughter. I sit on the couch wondering if and when I'll feel something. The past five nights since his death, I've lain in bed at night and made shopping lists, mentally rearranged my living room back in Virginia. I feel guilty because I can't cry.

Now I leaf through scrapbooks, looking for clues to tell me who my father was. A Post Office co-worker of my father's has stopped by to offer condolences. I make him sit beside me; I tell him about each person in every photo, when and where the picture was taken. I can't stop chattering. As my father would say, it's like my tongue's been vaccinated with a phonograph needle. Maybe it's easier to talk to a stranger, someone I don't have to see again.

*****

This one is of our dog, Butch. You can see from the photo, he's nothing in particular. We thought he was beautiful. He was halfway between a small dog and a big dog, I guess a middling dog, with thick black fur, a tiny white triangle under his muzzle, and big brown eyes.

We got Butch from our neighbors, the Santmyers, before I was born. Mr. Santmyer had trained Butch to hunt when he was a puppy. Opening day of Massachusetts deer season, Mr. Santmyer would whistle, bang the hood of his truck with his fist, and he and Butch would be gone three days. My father said this ticked Mrs. Santmyer off, since hunting season usually fell over Thanksgiving.

"*Him out there in the woods,*" my father grinned, "*living on peanut butter and whiskey, her stuck cooking Thanksgiving dinner for his whole fam damly.*" I giggled whenever he said that, "*fam damly.*"

Daddy said, "*That dog would scent a rabbit and take off like you'd starved him a month.*"

He told us how Mr. Santmyer followed behind, raising his rifle when he came up on Butch, who stood pointing, his whole body quivering.

"*Good work, Butch,*" Mr. Santmyer would say, patting him on the head.

Butch would look back over his shoulder, as if to say, "*Shoot, you damn idiot!*" But Mr. Santmyer always put his gun down. Though he loved to hunt, he couldn't bear to kill anything, so hunting season was a mixture of joy and exasperation for Butch.

Mrs. Santmyer brought Butch over to our house one night soon after Mr. Santmyer died, saying, "*I'm too old to take care of him any more.*"

My father didn't hunt. It took Butch awhile to get used to doing without. When my mother let him out, mornings, he'd cut through the woods to my grandmother Gracie's house, or roam down back by Hitchins' swamp. Every so often, he'd come back stinking from having rolled in something dead and we'd have to shut him out at night until the smell wore off.

Since he wasn't allowed to beg at meals, Butch slept on the kitchen floor beside the table. My parents would drink coffee after supper, while us kids cleared the round oak table and washed the dishes. They would talk about Butch as if he were someone they had met on the street that afternoon. "*Ooooh, what a handsome animal. What beautiful fur. And those eyes! What a good-looking beast!*"

Though he kept his eyes closed, a little smirk would appear on Butch's face. Now, I know people think dogs don't smile, but they're wrong. My father ooohed and aahhhed; Butch covered his ears and eyes with his paws, as if embarrassed at so much praise. When he couldn't stand it any longer, he would roll onto his back and stick his legs straight up in the air. My father would reach out a foot and scratch his dog belly. Daddy loved Butch the most, more than he loved the cats; more than we loved Butch, even. And—so it seemed to me then—more than he loved us.

When I was little, Butch went everywhere with me, growling at anyone who came too close. He did the same with my little brother Michael when he started walking.

Nobody hugged in our house, but everybody fawned over the animals. Mumma would dress Butch up in my brother's baby clothes, take him up in her arms in the maple rocker, and sing to him: "*Rock a bye baby, in the treetop, when the wind blows, the cradle will rock.*" Butch would sit up straight in her lap, some dumb baby bonnet on his head, and howl along. Those were the only times I heard my mother sing, the two of them rocking and singing and howling together.

I dream that our family sits on straight-backed wooden chairs in our living room, only the room is huge, like a football stadium. My mother, my father, my sister Lizzie, my older brother Brother, my little brother Michael, and me, on hard chairs, a row of us on straight-backed hard chairs tipped against the walls. A black lake fills the middle of the living room. Nobody speaks; we stare, as if hypnotized. Slowly, my father reaches out a pale white arm. We each reach out. Our arms grow longer, our waxy fingers stretching thinner and thinner, until they reach all the way to Butch, and our cats, Midnight and Peter, curled on an island made of mother's hand-braided wool rug floating in the middle of the black lake in our living room. My mother murmurs to our pets. We all murmur, cooing and crooning to our pets, tickling them, rubbing them behind their ears. Babytalk forms a buzzing cloud, it hangs gray over the lake. We sit there, chairs tipped back against the walls, arms outstretched, staring straight ahead, murmuring to our animals, far apart from each other.

I still dream this dream sometimes, usually when something is wrong and I'm trying not to know it.

We always had Butch and two cats, different cats over the years. If one got run over by a car or something, Dr. Hitchins would bring us a new one. Dr. Hitchins was our neighbor, a veterinarian with a quiet voice and a crinkly *Father Knows Best* smile. Sometimes I would pretend to myself that I was his little girl. My mother told me once that when I was a baby, Dr. and Mrs. Hitchins offered to adopt me, saying they would see to it I went to the best schools, that I would be good company for their boy, Ritchie. "*We may not be rich like certain people,*" Mumma sniffed, "*but we can take care of our own.*" That was the closest my mother ever came to saying out loud that she loved me.

Anyway, I was eight when our cat Midnight died from kidney stones. Dr. Hitchins said there wasn't anything we could do, just keep her comfortable. She slept slung across the toilet seat, front paws on one side, back paws on the other, suspended over the bowl. This worked real well, except when somebody had to go.

Just a few weeks after Midnight died, somebody poisoned Ragmop, my favorite cat of all time. He was a genuine Maine Coon cat, grey, with loose fur you could pull away from his body like a bloodhound's. That Saturday, he crawled into our yard toward the house. Nobody was home but me. I called Dr. Hitchins; it rang and rang and rang at his house. I hung up. I didn't know what to do. I sat on the ground beside Ragmop and pulled him into my lap. He moaned the way Brother moaned the time his eardrum broke. I tugged on Ragmop's ears the special way he liked. I said, "*It's all right, Ragmop, don't cry.*" I patted him and cried with him and sang him all the songs I knew, until he died.

The next week, Dr. Hitchins brought us tiny brother and sister kittens. We named them Peter and Wendy, for Peter Pan. Peter was orange striped. Wendy was black, with a black and white nose divided down the middle.

If Butch so much as wagged his tail, a kitten leapt on it. Mumma said they were good for him, he was getting old. He held them down with a giant paw, licking them like a good mother. They slept curled together against his side. We would call, "*Get the kitten, Butch!*" and

Butch would rush around the house, nose to the ground, until he found one. Taking it up with his teeth, lips curled back as if carrying one of Gracie's porcelain teacups, he would plunk down a soggy furball at our feet, wagging his tail proudly.

We were in the kitchen after breakfast one late March morning, laughing at Peter and Wendy as they chased each other in and out around Butch's legs. Wendy stopped to chew on a pork bone in Butch's dish. Butch snapped, faster than you can think.

But instead of backing off, Wendy fell over. She twitched on the floor like a fly you've hit too lightly with a fly-swatter. Butch turned to us; the look in his eyes was awful.

Daddy bolted from the room, returning seconds later with the snow broom. We crowded around Wendy, whose eyes were up in her head now, her face moving fast.

"*Get back!*" he yelled. He leaned over close to Wendy.

"*Her back's broken,*" he said, straightening up.

We looked at him, at Wendy. Daddy raised the broom handle and brought it down on her. She lay still.

Daddy grabbed Butch up by the collar. "*Bastard!*" he yelled, hitting him with the broom. "*You bastard! You bastard!*" He dragged Butch to the back door, yanking the door open with one hand, throwing him down the steps. Butch ran into the woods behind our house.

We stood looking down at Wendy, who didn't move. My father knelt and wrapped her in a white towel. Her head tilted limply in his palm; there was no blood on the towel. As Daddy came back inside, we heard howling from the woods. It wasn't like a dog howling at the moon, short, quick yips. It was long and steady, keening, one note, then stop; then start up again.

That night in bed, I listened to Butch out there in the woods, his low wail like a train whistle in the distance. I wanted to wail with him. I let tears run down my face, but I was afraid to blow my nose. They might yell, "*I hear any more crying in there, I'll give you something to cry about.*" Instead, I whispered into the dark, "*You're a good boy, Butch; you're a good boy.*"

It did not occur to me to go into the woods after Butch, to search for my friend, cradle him in my arms. I guess I believed that what had happened was between Butch and Daddy, that anything I might do would break something, their friendship, Daddy's pride, something.

Daddy was usually at the Post Office by the time we got up, but next morning when I came into the kitchen, he was sitting at the table with Mumma.

"*I lost my temper, Ruth. I just lost my temper,*" he said to her. "*You know I never hit animals.*"

This was true. For all Daddy's explosions and Mumma's beatings, I never saw either of them strike an animal. The best sense I could make of it then was that maybe they believed you had to hit kids to change them, but that an animal just *is*, unalterable, born full blown without a chance at heaven, so to hit one would be only cruel.

Daddy got up from the table. On the way back with the coffee, he opened the door and looked out. A few minutes later, he went to the refrigerator for canned milk, then opened the back door again, calling, "*Buuutch! Here Butch, good boy.*" There was a fake lightness in his voice, as if this were just any day, and he were calling Butch in for breakfast. He whistled three long whistles, Butch's signal. The howling did not stop. Daddy shut the door just short of slamming it, then sat back down.

"*God damn it, Ruth, I couldn't see straight, it made me so mad, seeing that kitten hurt.*"

"*I know, Carver,*" she said. "*I know.*"

Nobody mentioned the howling at supper. We acted hypernormal, as if there was a dead fish on the dining room table and we were trying to eat, pretending it wasn't there. We did that a lot in my family, ate our way around a lot of stinking dead fish.

After supper, my father sat at the newly-wiped table staring out into the dark yard as if he thought he could see Butch if he came home. When I went to bed he was still there. I covered my head with my pillow to shut out the sound.

The next afternoon, out the bathroom window, I saw Daddy walk into the forest alone. He never went into the woods except to dig up wild lady's-slippers to transplant into our yard, or to get pine mulch. A couple minutes later, I heard him, calling, "*Buuutch! Heeeere, Butch! C'mon, Butch, here boy.*" Then the three long whistles. The howling stopped for a minute, maybe while Butch moved to a new spot, maybe just out of Daddy's sight behind the trees. Then it began again, and Daddy whistled again.

After a long while, Daddy came back inside. He went down to the cellar, where he worked until supper, pounding, with the radio on loud.

The next day we continued to pretend not to hear Butch. He sounded hoarse, like I feel when my throat is sore. Mumma didn't yell at us all day; Daddy didn't crack one pun or make a sarcastic comment. Lizzie and Brother and I got on each other's nerves more than usual; I even started a pinching fight with little Michael, whom I usually protected from the others.

Mumma made clam chowder for supper, so I set the table with bowls, butter, and a plate of oyster crackers. Counting big spoons from the silverware drawer, I saw a shadow out the window. I ran to the cellar steps. "*Daddy,*" I called, "*Butch is back!*"

He came up the steps fast. But instead of going to the back door, he walked to the window. "*Shhh,*" he said, as if Butch could hear us, "*Let him come in on his own.*"

Butch was hard to see in the twilight. He stood at the edge of the yard, watching the house. Then he slipped behind our Navy hammock, past the peastone clothes yard, disappearing in and out of shadow. He came alongside the bulkhead and stopped at the bottom step. He stood there, black fur melting into the fast-coming night.

Daddy walked to the door and peered through the little window at the top, as if suddenly shy. He opened the door carefully. "*Hi, boy,*" he said in his bedtime-story voice, "*Want some breakfast?*"

Butch didn't move. Daddy propped the door open and walked away. Butch stood there. Looking stiffly to his left, then to his right, he placed a paw on the bottom step, and started up the four steps to the top. His legs shook as he climbed, like an old man's.

His matted fur was wet; it seemed to me to have lost color. He stood on the top landing, looking, watching Daddy's back as he reached to pour dry food into Butch's bowl. After what seemed forever, Butch walked over to his bowl and started eating.

The next three days, Butch wouldn't come out of the basement. Once I snuck down there; he was sleeping, turned away from me. Daddy said, "*Leave him be,*" so I didn't go down again.

We were eating supper the third night when Butch appeared at the top of the cellar stairs, his big head filling the doorway. No one said anything. He walked across the kitchen floor, and dropped down with a "*thunk*" in his spot beside the table. No one spoke. Then he rolled over and stretched his legs straight up in the air. Daddy reached out a foot and rubbed Butch's belly.

After that, we all took up again like it had never happened.

*****

I don't know what listening to me that afternoon did for the guy from the Post Office—I never saw him again—but I felt better, getting words out. The numbness lasted for months, as if I had run out of gas, but had get down a steep hill. With the motor off, I could coast. When my feelings came back, it took another couple years for me to forgive my father for dying on me before I could get to know him, before he knew me.

I'll tell you a secret. It was only after he died that I got to know my father. We're good friends now. I talk to him in my head, ask him questions. *"Were you ever this scared?" "You were so smart, did it break your heart when you couldn't go to college?" "How did you feed us all on a mailman's pay?"*

I get answers. Oh, not actual words; more like pictures, certain feelings. I understand now that my father was scared most of his life, that his rages hid his fear. I know how he felt as he was dying—something we could never speak of while he was alive. Don't ask me to explain how this works. I can only tell you, I'm not crazy. A wheel doesn't turn part-way, then stop, just because someone dies. It's never too late to make peace. Heart relationships go on forever.

Joseph Cornell made a name in art with small boxes of dried flowers, cut outs, and faded theater tickets. He was much enamored of ballerinas. The Prima Donna Toumanova remembers he took five steps backward when they met, and when he died, his sister recalls his final words, *"I only wish I had not been so reserved."*

LOVE AT FIRST SIGHT I

I have made so many of these
art boxes. Dried flowers, theater
tickets, bits of lace. I am glad
when someone decides not
to buy one.

This one costs a lot, because of
the feathers. See how the light
glints off the indigo
shafts, as if off watered
silk, or oil?

One day I found a bird
hidden in the woods, set
in ferns like a jewel in velvet;
her wound was hidden.

She shook, one eye
cocked at me. I felt clumsy,
a loud giant; I took five steps
backward to grant privacy.
I wanted to warm her
in my hands; an awkward
man like me, I might
have crushed her.

I imagined her heart
pulsing in my cupped
palms, warm to warm.
I held my hands behind
my back so they would not
reach out.

I imagined my lips
brushing her feathers.
I closed my throat
against crooning.
I willed myself invisible.

She shivered a long time,
looking at me. Then she chirped,
once, louder than you would
expect from a small thing.

Days later I returned
to find her feathers, fallen
in a blueblack nest
about her. I wish I could have
touched her downy lightness
to my cheek. I wonder if
I could have saved her. I wonder
if she could have saved me.
I only wish
I had not been so reserved.

LOVE AT FIRST SIGHT II

The giant is my father, I am
the bird; I am the giant
and he is the bird. He lays
dying in a hospital
bed, strapped to tubes, unable
to talk. His eyes
look at me in terror.
I watch from the doorway,
five steps back,
withholding kisses for kisses withheld,
in terror of my own rage and love.
Until I die I will
wish I had not been
so reserved. I will wish
I had held his hand.

THE MAN IN THE PICTURE

AMY BIANCOLLI

ON A SHELF IN my living room sits a 3 × 5 photo, black and white, circa 1945, of a man in a snap-brim hat. He is smashingly handsome: vital, laughing, in his late 30s or early 40s, his curved Roman nose anchoring the heavy features of his face. His arms are crossed; his hat is tipped; his bow tie is sassy, polka-dotted and crisp.

It is approaching a year since my father died, and I am still transfixed by his photo. I am transfixed not because I see in it some soft reminder of the man I knew, but because I see no reminder at all. He isn't there. I regard it as I might the candid shot of a golden-era movie star, some distant but intriguing personality whose charisma gripped the camera and commandeered passage to the present day. Who was this? I ask myself, studying his smile and seeing in it vague hints of my own. What was he doing? Was he at work? Out on the town? And why was he laughing? Whoever he was, whatever he meant to the people who knew him, the man in the photo had disappeared years before I learned he was ever there. Only now, in the long, numb months since his death, have I started to get to know him.

My father was 56 when I was born. Two and a half years later, he retired, leaving behind almost four decades as a classical music critic for *The New York World-Telegram & Sun.* He'd been highly regarded in music and newspaper circles, admired for his lively prose and his reluctance—even refusal—to ruin someone's career with a vitriolic review. He was known for his scholarship, his athleticism, his fascination with linguistics, his generosity, his Italian roots, his love of opera, the baker's dozen of books he'd published, his amateur boxing, and his manic, heavy-handed way with a typewriter. He had a reputation for breaking manuals.

The man I knew was older, frailer, less sure of himself and the world. He was 85 when he died, and the last fifteen years had been difficult and slow. Alzheimer's had nibbled away at his memory and made it first uncomfortable, then impossible for him to keep up with friends who knew him in his prime. He stopped writing. He stopped listening to music. After a while he even stopped reading, focusing all of his mental energy on crossword puzzles. When I went away to college I wrote him long and frequent letters, and he did his best to write back—always in huge, block-like handwriting, rarely more than a page. Some time later he ceased trying, just as he had ceased trying to keep up with the conversations that whirled around him like fallen leaves on a windy day. He forgot faces, names, ideas. He forgot the first half of a sentence by the time he'd heard the last. He forgot so much, in fact, that when my sister committed suicide—a few months before his own death—my mother and I decided not to tell him, realizing, with sadness and relief, that he wouldn't remember it anyway.

My father never knew me as an adult. In his final years, while I was thrashing out a career in journalism, he was receding further and further behind the divider. I longed to tell him about my work, about the changes in the newspaper industry since he'd retired, about my breathless explorations into new writers and composers. I wanted to tell him about myself—who I was, what sort of woman I'd become, who my friends were and what my life was—but I couldn't. I was Amy, *Amigita*, his little friend from long ago. I was not the person who grew up and went to college and graduate school and got married and found her greatest professional joy doing exactly what her father had done for a living. I was the daughter who loved him— that was enough, and that was all. The rest he forgot. Even my husband, whom he greatly admired, was greeted always as a kind but nameless gentleman, that strong young man who appeared with his daughter and enveloped him in hugs. In my father's eyes, it was all a blur. And so was I.

I wasn't there when he died. He had broken his hip—and, somewhere along the line, suffered a heart attack—and for weeks afterward I drove back and forth, Albany to Connecticut, Connecticut to Albany, fearing that every visit with him would be the last. We knew he was dying and said good-bye many times. Only half aware, his attention fixed firmly on the next world, he accepted our farewells in silence and awaited the end with sweet-natured distraction. When it came I was at a friend's house-warming party in Albany, chatting about music in the fresh heat of a June sun. My husband, who'd gone home to do some work, returned earlier than expected and quietly pulled me aside. He said the words and I cried, then told my father that I loved him and thanked God for him and hoped he was all right. It felt odd to address him directly and know that everything I said would, at last, be understood. He wouldn't forget a word.

In the days that followed I spoke to him more and more. Late one night before the funeral I left my mother's house and sat on the damp, cool lawn, watching ripples of light skate across the lake below. I thought of my father, not of his last days, but of the man I'd glimpsed as a child before he retreated into the fog. I remembered that father. I remembered the fears I'd shared with him, the arguments we'd had, the interest he once took in my life and the pleasure that crossed his face when I snagged a baseball from the air and threw it swiftly back. ("One-hand bip!" he'd yell, using a name he'd earned as a youngster. "Look at that! One-hand bip!")

That night I told him everything. I told him about my husband, our wedding, the rewards and challenges since then. I told him about my work as an arts writer and music critic; I told him how proud I was to be his daughter and how often people I interviewed asked me if I was related to "the New York critic . . . Louis Biancolli." I told him about my love of music, which had exploded since his Alzheimers had taken hold, and I described the hard but happy task of learning the violin. I told him I played in an orchestra and taught writing part-time at a nearby college. I told him I liked to jog, and bike, and feel my own strength, as he did at my age. I told him about the novel I'd written, the new work I'd started, the movies I'd seen, the books I'd read and the eccentricities I'd developed. I told him I had a gray streak in my hair. I told him that my friends seemed to value me and that I liked to make them laugh. I told him I'd inherited his taste for chocolate. I liked to eat. I liked to dance. I tried to be a good Catholic. I loved my mother and husband. I missed my sister. I missed him.

Did he hear me? I believe so, yes. And he has heard me on many occasions since then, as I've huddled over my reporter's notebook in one concert hall or another, trying to find just the right word to describe that pianist's phrasing. Daddy, help me. "*Fluid,*" *Amigita. Write "fluid,*" he says, or I say to myself in the voice I'm always able to conjure. And as the months go by it's a younger voice, a stronger voice. I look at an empty seat two rows ahead and I imagine him sitting there—alert, focused, his hair the shiny salt and pepper of my childhood, not the thick white brush that I last saw. He is an old man no longer.

Bit by bit, I am forming a new relationship with my father. It isn't easy; for years I had treated him not as a fellow adult but as a child, as someone less capable than I, less aware, less equipped to cope with the world and its byzantine rules. And I hated it. I will never forget my father's second cataract operation, when he returned from the hospital bandaged and blind and warned, by his doctors, not to lean over under any circumstances. If he did, the tiny stitches holding in his eye's new lens would pop, rendering him permanently sightless. I had taken off the week to help my mother, and between the two of us we held watch over my father all night for five nights, sitting next to his bed with a stack of murder mysteries at our feet. Every hour or so my father would wake, rise as if it were morning and spot some speck on the floor that deserved close inspection. He would lean to pick it up, and I or my mother would jump to attention. "Stop it!" I screamed, over and over. "Daddy! *Don't!* Do you want to go blind?!" And he, his face crumpled with hurt and confusion, turned to me and asked: "Amy. Why are you yelling at your father?" I don't know. I don't know.

It's been hard to let go of my old father, to bid farewell to his gentle, shuffling presence here on earth. I loved him as he was. Yet as I say good-bye, I am struck by the emergence of another father, the one whose books line my wall, whose long career echoes in every whisper of my own. How often I stumble across something he wrote—on a record jacket, a program, in a magazine—and wonder at his facility with words. Though his old age passed with death, his youth remains in his work. I read it and hear my father, full, alive, singing with confidence and vigor.

The man in the photo waits on my shelf, laughing. I search his face and find there not the ghost of a person I never knew but the birth of someone new, someone whose strength and humor carry me through my grief. He offers a hand of friendship, and I grasp.

THIS IS GEORGE
CONSTANCE SCHRAFT

AWAKE AT THREE O'CLOCK one humid morning, I climbed out of bed, leaving my husband Terry's side. It was the last week of August, and the city was stifling. I wandered through the apartment, the wood floor cool and smooth beneath my feet. The day before, despite the heat, I'd gotten down on my knees to wash and buff it.

In the study I opened a book by C. S. Lewis that a friend had given me when my mother died six weeks earlier. I opened to the first page.

> "No one ever told me that grief felt so like fear. I am not afraid, but the sensation is like being afraid. The same fluttering in the stomach. The same restlessness, the yawning. I keep swallowing."

Closing the book, I walked to the front window and stared down at the grey, deserted street. I disagreed with Mr. Lewis. I was afraid.

On his way to work that morning Terry dropped our two-year-old Nick at the babysitter's. Left alone, I sat at the kitchen table drinking tea. The fact of my mother's death was finally settling in, I supposed, which explained my lethargy. The day before, I'd forced myself to clean the gritty floors. Today it seemed unlikely that I would accomplish anything.

I made some phone calls but reached only a string of answering machines. Everyone I knew seemed to be out of town. I called the house in northern Connecticut that my older sister Anna and her husband had rented for the last two weeks of summer, but no one answered. On that hot, bright day, everyone had to be at the beach.

My younger sister Colette was in Connecticut, too. She'd driven up with our father for Labor Day weekend; at the last minute, she'd persuaded him to go. Usually eager to travel, especially somewhere he'd never been before, he'd been reluctant since our mother died. Until this trip, he hadn't gone anywhere but to the hospital where he worked. His reticence to travel was the only sign of his grief, though. From the moment he'd gone upstairs to waken her from a nap and found that she was dead, he'd been in control. Following his lead, we all were.

At one o'clock, I picked up Nick and brought him home for his nap. Accustomed to our routine, he didn't fuss when I boosted him into his crib.

As I was sitting down at the table again with my umpteenth cup of tea, the telephone rang. It was exactly when my mother used to call, knowing that Nick would be asleep and I'd have time to chat. Though immediately tearful at the thought of her, I eagerly picked up the phone. It was the first time it had rung all day.

Before I had a chance to say hello, Colette said, "I'm sorry. We were just—and he went under—" Her voice was racing and indistinct.

"What?"

"He went under," she repeated.

"Who?"

"Dad."

"He drowned?"

"No. He—I don't know—his heart."

Mysteriously, the panic and sadness of the past few days disappeared, and I waited calmly in the dim kitchen, the extra-long telephone cord wound tightly around my index finger.

Anna came on the phone. "We're at the hospital. They've got him on the respirator. His heart was stopped at least ten minutes. It's no use. He's not going to be the same, and he'd hate that, you know he'd hate that—"

"Shut up," I said, not angrily, because I needed quiet.

After telling her that I'd get there as soon as I could, I went to the bedroom closet, pulled a suitcase off the shelf, and filled it with clothes. I put on a dress that I'd bought several years earlier and never worn. I didn't know why I was bothering to change out of my shorts, until I remembered my mother sitting in the waiting room of the hospital a few years earlier, composed and impeccable in a woolen suit and blue silk blouse. My father's gall bladder had ruptured earlier that morning, and seeing her dressed up, I'd been annoyed. When she had called to tell me that he was in surgery, I'd hurried out of my apartment without even showering. At the time I hadn't understood why she had gone to the trouble of dressing up; now I knew that she was believing that he would live. If he was going to die, what would it have mattered how she looked?

Nick turned over in his sleep. I'd forgotten about him. Picking up the telephone, I dialed Terry's office, I had to make plans. I had to get moving.

Terry's secretary told me that he'd just left.

"Where was he going? I have to reach him. My father—"

"I know. Nora, I'm so sorry. Your brother-in-law called here. Terry's on his way home."

Contemplating a long stay in Connecticut while my father recuperated, I wondered if I should go there by myself. I hesitated, then called the airlines for flight information. The closest airport was at least an hour from the small hospital that my father had been taken to. I dialed the train station. While listening to a recording, I made notes, jotting down things I didn't want to forget. The cat. I had to remember to leave out plenty of food.

Terry arrived, tear-stained, a wreck. He put his arms around me and started to console me. "I can't believe it. I'm so sorry. It's impossible."

I pulled away. "He's going to be all right. The cardiac surgeon up there wants to try something else, something to do with Dad's pacemaker. You never saw him after open-heart surgery. He was barely alive, but he made it. He always makes it."

Terry shook his head, took the portable phone from me, and walked into the living room, dialing. I swung around and started back to the bedroom. I heard Terry say, "Dad—Bill's dying."

Annoyed, I threw my bathing suit into the suitcase, zipped it closed, and tiptoed into Nick's room to pack his things.

By the time I came up front, Terry had calmed himself. He went to the parking garage for the car. While he was gone, I called the house in Connecticut for directions to the hospital. Anna's husband Ben answered. He was home with my niece and nephew. Hearing me, he began to cry.

"Don't," I said, only slightly more gently than I'd spoken to Terry.

"Anna did her best—she gave him CPR on the beach—but he was already gone—he was blue."

"He's going to be fine," I said. To me, it seemed obvious that my father couldn't die with my mother hardly gone. It wasn't the way things worked.

Terry carried the suitcase, filled with what the three of us would have needed for a vacation. I lifted Nick from the crib, holding his head to my heart. When he was born, when the doctor first lay him on my chest, Nick had wailed and I patted him awkwardly. "Keep a rhythm," the delivery nurse advised me. "Like the heart beat. Ba-boom ba-boom ba-boom."

As I was securing Nick in his car seat, he wakened. While Terry drove, I read books. "Again," Nick would say, and instead of distracting him with something else, the way I usually did, I read the same three books over and over. By the time we'd reached the outskirts of the city, I realized that Nick had memorized them. When I read the first half of a sentence, he could finish it.

"'This is—'"

"George," said Nick.

"'He lived in—'"

"Africa."

"'He was—'"

"A good little monkey."

"'And always—'"

"Very curious," Nick finished.

"That's incredible," I said. "Terry, did you hear that?"

Around the time that we crossed the border into Connecticut, I said, "I have a good feeling."

"I don't think you should get your hopes up," said Terry.

"This is a warning," I went on. "From now on, Dad's got to take it easy. We can't let him chase after the kids. And he's got to watch what he eats. No more peanut butter on saltines before bed."

"I really don't think you should be thinking this way."

I sat back. For the moment, Nick was content looking out the window at the other cars. I remembered a night—I must have been about ten—when I couldn't sleep, and I slipped out of bed and down the hall to my parents' room. My mother was asleep, but the light was still on. I went down the front stairs and found my father at his desk in the study.

Hearing me, he looked up and smiled. I told him that I couldn't sleep. I knew why: my class was going on a trip the next day and, prone to carsickness, I was nervous that I would throw up on the bus.

My father pushed back his chair, stood up and took my hand. "Right this way," he said.

In the kitchen he filled two bowls with cereal, and we sat across from each other at the table. He ate his shredded wheat with gusto, bending over to spoon up the last milk-soaked square. Then he went and got the peanut butter and a box of crackers from the pantry.

Afterward, he opened the back door, and the dog bounded in, his tags jingling, his toenails clattering on the linoleum. My father locked the door, checked that the garage door was lowered, then turned out the kitchen lights. As we moved through the house, he checked more doors, turned out more lights, synchronized the hall clock, which always ran slow, with his watch. He hummed. It was after midnight, but he showed no sign of being tired. He could as easily have been starting his day.

Upstairs he stopped in the bathroom for a towel. Once I was in bed, he fanned me with it, the way a harem boy would, silently and rhythmically. He whispered, "Close your peepers," and then I was asleep.

Just past New Haven, Terry pulled off the highway at a rest stop for gas and a snack for Nick. When I called the house for news, Ben answered, his voice flat.

"He's gone."

I crumpled the page of directions to the hospital and took down another set to the house, not at all confident that I was getting them right. After hanging up, I stayed by the phone, from where I could see Terry and Nick sharing a packet of French fries at an outside table. I reached into my pocketbook, which was bulging; in my haste to get ready, I'd kept stuffing things into it.

When I located my address book, I dialed my mother's sister. I called her because she was religious, and I thought she might be able to say something that would help. But when I told her that my father was dead, she said, "Thank God."

Afterward, I found out that my sisters had already called her, so she knew the condition that our father was in. She was glad that he had died, rather than continue to hang on with life support systems. But when she said, "Thank God," I hung up.

Again, I stared out the window at my husband and my son, whom I adored, I reminded myself. Past them was the parking lot; past the parking lot was the highway, and beyond that, the unseeable horizon.

I insisted on driving the rest of the way.

When my mother died, there were sirens and the telephone ringing and friends of the family coming and going. With my father, there was the hum of the highway and Nick's prattle.

Occasionally Terry asked if I was sure that I was all right. Yes, I said each time. Although I could tell that he didn't believe me, it was the truth. I was all right, just blank, as after a hot, windy day at the beach.

By the time that Terry, Nick, and I reached the house in Connecticut, it was late in the evening. My sisters were on their second bottle of wine and more or less incoherent. Terry carried Nick upstairs and put him to bed. Colette opened every cupboard in the kitchen before finding me a wine glass. Then she and Anna and I went outside to the patio.

"Why didn't you wait for me?" I asked.

"He was gone," said Anna. "Just the machines were keeping him going."

"You should be glad you didn't have to see him that way," Colette added.

I heard Terry and Ben talking inside. When I'd told Terry the news, he had cried again, and I said, "Just stop."

"We better make a list," Anna said. Like our father, she was in the habit of keeping lists, on the backs of envelopes, sales slips, bank statements.

She went inside and rummaged in the kitchen, returning with a yellow legal pad. We began with a list of people to contact. Anna and Colette had already reached our closest relatives and our father's best friends who would spread the news. But there were his out-of-town friends and our own friends. There was the church. We had to arrange for a funeral. We had to call the undertaker. We had to call our father's lawyer, and the medical school to which years ago our father had arranged to donate his body.

"What about an obituary?" I said.

Turning to a fresh page, Anna began jotting down the facts of our father's life. He was 69 years old. He was born in East Orange, New Jersey. His mother's maiden name was Duttweiler. He attended Cornell University and New York Medical College. He was a captain in the Army. Anna made a note to call the hospital for his professional affiliations. He was survived by three daughters.

"What about Mom?" Colette said. "We have to mention Mom."

Anna wrote, "His wife was the late—" and pushed aside the pad. She had filled a page with facts about our father, but they were no more than a skeleton, completely inadequate to show the sort of person he was. His profession—he was a pathologist—seemed all wrong. By definition, it seemed to deny his sense of humor, his energy, his genuine interest in people.

There was no mention that for sixty-nine years, our father had lived with a congenital heart condition that might have made an invalid of a less potent man. There was no mention of his laugh, of his signature feather bow ties, of how he had faced the world—chest back, arms open.

Anna poured herself more wine. "Am I drunk enough to pass out, do you think?" she asked. "Poor Daddy, all alone in the morgue."

I pushed forward my glass. Anna missed, pouring wine over my hand and the table. I longed for my father's hands, the familiar liver spots and wrinkles. I longed for his skinny legs, the smell of his hair tonic, the line of scars that began at his left collar bone where his pacemaker had been inserted, traveled down the middle of his chest, then veered right where his gall bladder had been removed.

Anna said, "He looked beautiful, sprawled out on the beach in his tiny little Speedo."

Hearing the panic in her voice, I realized that like me, she was going to suffer from having loved him too much.

"I'm glad we came," Colette said. "He had a really great time here. He played softball with a bunch of kids down the street yesterday, and he took a bike ride this morning. Both nights we went out for lobster."

"He wasn't supposed to run around like that," I said. "He definitely shouldn't have had lobster two nights in a row."

Anna suddenly seemed less drunk. "What did you want his last meal to be—filet of sole?"

When the telephone rang a little after midnight, the three of us did not move. Terry came out to tell us that it was Colette's boyfriend

Luke, who had come by train to be with her. Luke had called for the address; he was taking a taxi cab from the station.

Colette got up and started inside.

I didn't want anyone to move. If we didn't move, time wouldn't move. I wanted us to stay together in the salty chill of the night, damp beach towels around our shoulders. I remembered from when our mother died, that now, with the shock and the adrenaline, was the best we were going to feel for a while. By sleeping, we'd move to a day he'd never lived. We'd begin our life without him.

"Where are you going?" I asked Colette.

"To pack."

"What do you mean?"

"I'm leaving. I'm going to drive Dad's car home."

"But Luke just got off the train—"

Colette slipped past the screen door that she'd been holding open with her hip.

"I'm going to talk to her," I said to Anna.

Anna shrugged, a fresh cigarette between her lips, and bent forward to light a match.

"She shouldn't drive. She's been drinking."

Terry touched my arm. "Nora, maybe you shouldn't—"

I took the stairs two at a time. They were steep and narrow, and I tripped near the top, banging my knee and elbow. I limped down the hallway. Not knowing the configuration of rooms, I listened for Colette and finally found her in a small room with bunk beds.

She was bent over the lower one, zipping her overnight bag. When she straightened, she said, "I have to get out of here."

"It seems strange, that's all, Luke just getting here and you turning around and leaving."

She silently hoisted the bag onto her shoulder. She was the first to understand that we weren't bound by any rules anymore. When she moved past me, I had the feeling that our roles had been reversed, that I was the little sister. Colette's footsteps resounded on the stairs.

Someone had made coffee. We stood around the kitchen, drinking it. In the quiet, I could hear the clatter of the waves falling back over the pebbly beach a block away, soon echoed by the cab pulling onto the gravel driveway.

Anna turned to Colette and said, "Are you sure this is what you really want to do, sweetheart?"

It was our father's line, what he would say when one of us went to him for permission after our mother had said no. Colette nodded and brusquely said good-bye. We followed her outside. She spoke briefly to Luke, then headed down the street toward where our father's car was parked. Surprised but acquiescent, Luke quickly shook our hands, then trotted after her.

"Shouldn't we do something?" I said.

The question was rhetorical. Hardly was Luke inside the car before Colette took off. The street was narrow, with cars parked on either side. She managed to maneuver out safely and still leave us with the impression that we'd heard a crash.

Terry and I were assigned the attic room, where my father had been staying, and before getting into bed, I packed his shorts and shirts in his suitcase. I found the book that he'd been reading—a Dick Francis mystery, and I packed that, too.

The bed, a slice of foam rubber, was positioned directly below a skylight. I could have watched the stars, but instead, I curled into fetal position and tried not to breathe so fast. Beside me, Terry was silent. I waited for him to say something, but in a little while, I realized that he was asleep.

I took a breath and allowed my mind to close around what had happened. It hurt, but I knew that if I didn't do this, it would be worse. I'd learned during childbirth that if you accepted pain instead of fighting it, it was over sooner.

In labor with Nick, with the early contractions, this was easy. But later, when I was sweating and pacing or crumpled against a wall, trying to rest, it was more difficult to think of opening myself, when all I wanted was to give up and shut down. The times I succeeded in letting the contractions run their course, deeply and unimpeded, were literally breathtaking.

Like a tongue over a rough tooth, I explored the facts of my father's death. I pictured him waist-deep in the water, Anna's boy in his arms, then crumpling, holding the baby up as he sank. Did a light shine, or did the day gradually go dim, then black? Did he feel pain? Did he know, I wondered, that this was it? (My mother, everyone said, did not. She died in her sleep; when found, her body was in a relaxed position, her face slack, no sign of a struggle.)

Months later, I would say, "My father died in the Atlantic Ocean that he loved, with his family around, with a child in his arms." I would consider it a good way to die. But now, I rolled onto my back and saw that the night had clouded over.

I thought back to the morning, when the phone didn't ring, and I remembered when it finally did ring. I remembered the long car ride. "This is George. He lived in Africa." Arriving, I had hugged my sisters, who smelled of sweat and sunblock and wine. I'd felt like a fool in my dress.

Lying there, I wondered how Anna could have put my father in such an uncomfortable bed. I wondered if Colette and Luke had gotten home yet. I wondered what they had talked about during the ride and if they were in love, and I worried, if they one day decided to get married, who would give Colette away?

FATHER'S CHAIR WILL BE EMPTY

M E L I S S A   D R I B B E N

November 25, 1987

THANKSGIVING WAS MY FATHER'S holiday. He
delighted in it. This was the day to indulge himself in food and
surround himself with family.

He took pride in his candied yams, even though nearly everyone
else preferred theirs simply baked. His turnips were always the
creamiest. His pie crust was always the flakiest, and he refused to
throw in whole-wheat flour, despite pleadings from the health-
conscious contingent. Fiber had no place in this holiday, he'd say.
Bring on the sugar and butter.

"I should have been a chef," he'd say and then scold my mother
(whom he'd long ago usurped in the kitchen) for cluttering up the
spice shelf.

We humored his self-congratulatory mutterings. "Yes, Daddy," we'd say and be thankful, deep down, that he'd been able to earn a living as a photographer instead.

This year, his honored seat, a ladder-back armchair with a red cushion at the head of the table, will be empty.

We have missed him on many occasions this year—birthdays, anniversaries, and purely uneventful moments, like finding his rack of ties in the closet that my mother cannot bear to clean out. But Thanksgiving will be the day he will be missed most.

My father was a bear of a man, with thick hands and bushy brows, a man who loved to eat as much as cook. He piled his plate high, and everyone else's, too. He loved company in his excess. I can't say we minded.

In the days before we all became advocates of lean, he'd save the crisp turkey skin for my brother and me and sneak in an extra helping of stuffing for himself when my mother wasn't looking.

His anticipation of the gathering filled the house for days before the holiday. He'd wax the floors and wax the car. He'd give the dog a bath and polish the brass candlesticks. He'd replace his usual jug of cheap chablis with a bottle of Italian dry white.

It was only after his children had grown and left the house, I think, that he realized how much it meant to have his family huddled around him. His hugs had taken on a new intensity in recent years. I would bury my head in his ample chest, hold my breath, and let him fold around me.

When there were children in it once more, the house seemed replenished. My father would sit back into his armchair, at peace in the chaos—the grandchildren screeching, dogs barking, television booming. He was an optimist. When there was a lull in conversation, he'd ask, "Say something bright, intelligent, and cheerful." It was a routine he never tired of. "You're the greatest daddy in the world," we'd say, and he'd laugh. "You're giving me a snow job," he'd say, beaming in spite of himself.

When he was really in high spirits, he'd go into the top drawer of the dry sink and dust off his harmonica with the tortoise-shell skin. With a quivering hand to give the song lilt, he'd play something excruciatingly corny, like "Oh, Susanna."

During the last few years, since he had moved into semi-retirement, he had claimed the kitchen as his turf. He furnished the shelves with gadgets and modern machines—coffee grinder, pasta maker, microwave—and memorized the owner's manuals. A faithful student but no innovator, he'd follow recipes with biblical devotion.

It was little more than a year ago when the doctors told us, but not him, that he was dying of cancer, and that he would not live more than six months. We all posed for a final family portrait in the backyard. We all smiled tense smiles. Both my sister and I were pregnant, wondering if he'd ever see these two new grandchildren.

He didn't have much appetite for Thanksgiving last year, but he still managed to put away a second helping of turkey. He was bed-ridden by the time my sister's daughter was born in January. By March, he had lost 60 pounds. His embrace had lost its crushing force.

His hands were the only part of his body that had not wasted away; they seemed larger than ever in contrast to his bony arms. We never talked about his dying. I would sit beside him, watching television, and he'd reach for my hand and give it a gentle, lingering squeeze.

He died at the end of March, three days before my son was born.

This year, someone is going to have to learn how to carve the turkey and candy the yams.

FROM SWEET SUMMER: GROWING UP WITH AND WITHOUT MY DAD

BEBE MOORE CAMPBELL

THE DAY BEFORE MY father died I was a bridesmaid in my best friend's wedding and was staying with friends in Pittsburgh. My hostess awakened me around three or four o'clock Sunday morning and told me my uncle was on the phone. Uncle Norman's signature has always been brevity, an innate ability to get to the point with a minimum of fanfare or bullshit. When I picked up the phone he said, "Bebe, this is Norman. Your father died in a car accident this morning." Just like that. Then, "Did you hear me? Honey, did you hear Uncle Norman?"

A car accident, I thought, the phone still in my hand, Uncle Norman still talking, another car accident. That wasn't supposed to happen, is what ran through my mind. How did that happen twice in one life? Twice in two lives? Somehow, with the room spinning and my head aching, I listened to the rest of his instructions. I was to return home the next day and Uncle Cleat would take me to Richmond to identify the car and sign papers at the police station. We'd get Daddy's things at Mrs. Murphy's. Uncle Johnny, the eldest of Grandma Mary's eleven children, was having my father's body transported to North Carolina, where he would be buried in the family plot behind Grandma Mary's house. "He was coming to see you, Bebe," Uncle Norman said. "He didn't know you were out of town. You know your daddy, he just hopped in the car and got on the road. He was bringing a camera to take pictures of the baby."

When Uncle Norman said that, I remembered the pictures I'd promised to send Daddy weeks before and felt the first flicker of pain course through my body. Something swept through me, hot as lightning. All at once I was shaking and crying. God. He shouldn't have died like that, all alone out on a highway, slumped over the wheel like some fragile thing who couldn't take a good hard knock. God.

It was cool and dim in the funeral parlor, and filled with a strange odor I'd never smelled before. There were three rooms full of caskets—bronze, dark wood, light wood, pastels. A dizzying array. The funeral director was a friend of the family. Mr. Walson had an uncanny affinity for professional solemnity. He referred to Daddy as "the body." Did I wish to see the body? Was I satisfied with the appearance of the body? Did I care for knotty pine or cherry wood? He said this, his dark face devoid of all emotion, his expansive belly heaving threateningly against the dangerously thin belt around his waist. The same odd smell that filled the room clung to Mr. Walson. What was that smell? I leaned against Uncle Johnny and felt his hand on my shoulder. Upon learning that my grief was buttressed by a healthy insurance policy, Mr. Walson urged me to choose the cherry wood. I looked at Uncle Johnny questioningly; he has always known how to take charge. Maybe it comes from being the oldest. If he tells you to do something, you do it. "We'll take the cherry," he told the funeral director, who assured me he would take care of everything. But he could not, of course, take care of me. My grief was private and not covered.

As we left the funeral parlor, Uncle Johnny took my hand. "Do you know what your big-head daddy wanted to do?"

I shook my head.

"After I retired and moved down here next to Mama, he tried to talk me into doing some hog farming with him. Said we could make a lot of money. I told that joker, 'Man, I came down here to rest.'" Uncle Johnny looked at me. He was smiling. "Your daddy loved making money, didn't he, girl?"

"Loved it."

The cars rolled slowly up the unpaved lane that led to Grandma Mary's house, a fleet of Cadillacs, shiny, long and black, moving quietly, and stirring up dust that flew everywhere, clinging to everyone, coating shoes and suits and dresses, blowing in hair and on faces, where particles finally lodged in eyes that blinked, blinked, blinked then looked away.

It is still cool in North Carolina in April, a perfect time for a family reunion. Crowded in Grandma's yard were all the faces that looked like her face, the resemblance lying somewhere between the chin and the character lines that ran straight across high foreheads. There were others standing next to the ones who looked like her, so many people that their feet would have crushed Grandma's zinnias had they been in bloom.

The people looked up when the Cadillacs drove into the yard. They broke away from the joyous hugs of reunion, of North once again meeting South, put their cameras back into their bags and stood silently, at attention. The gray-haired old ladies fanned themselves with miscellaneous bits of paper, the backs of magazines, newspapers, napkins, even though it wasn't warm. All of a sudden there was a circle, shoulders touching, everyone's breath mingling into a giant sigh. Somebody, my daddy's first cousin, the preacher from New York, was praying, offering to the Lord brief, familiar words that the occasion called for: higher ground, no more suffering, home. The words fell around the crowd like soft pieces of flower petals. An old woman began to sing. The lyrics came back to the people who'd taken that long-ago bus ride from Pasquotank County to Philly, Jersey, New York, in heady rushes. All wiped the dust from their eyes and joined in. The last note had scarcely disappeared before Mr. Walson's assistants began calling the names of immediate family members and leading them to the limousines: ". . . Mr. and Mrs. John Moore, Mr. and Mrs. Elijah Moore." Grandma Mary gripped my fingers as I helped her into the car where my husband and daughter were waiting. I was about to sit down when I felt a hand on my back. I turned around. "How ya making out, kiddo?" It was Sammy, my Marine uncle, the hero of my childhood. Whenever I saw him I thought of starched uniforms, even though he hadn't been in the service for years.

"Okay, so far," I said. I took his hand.

He squeezed my fingers and helped me into the car. "I'm here if you need me," he said.

Later, when I was looking into the layers of expensive satin, blinking frantically as the top of the smooth cherry-wood coffin closed, it occurred to me that more than my father had passed away. Not only had I lost a treasured friend, but gone was the ease with which I could connect to his brothers, his male friends.

After he was buried, Grandma Mary's old friend Miss Lilly or Miss Lizzy, Miss Somebody, whose face had floated in and out of my childhood summers, a wiry woman with lines like railroad tracks on skin the color of a paper bag, put her hand in mine and whispered,

"Baby, you sho' put him away nice. Yes you did, chile," then, even more quietly, "God knows best, baby." She gave my arm three hard pats. Be . . . all . . . right. Don't. . . you . . . cry. Hush . . . baby . . . hush. I nodded to her, but later when I was alone I had a singular contemplation: his death wasn't for the best. That clear knowing hit me square upside my head after the last of the heavy North Carolina loam had covered the cherry-wood coffin, after Aunt Edith, my father's youngest sister, had heaved a final mournful wail that pierced through the surrounding fields of soybeans and corn that bordered my grandmother's house, then slowly faded. And what I felt wasn't even pain or grief. Just regret, gripping me like a steel claw.

In a way, it was like the end of an ordinary family reunion. I stood at the edge of the lane with Grandma Mary and watched the last of the out-of-town license plates careen down that narrow dirt road, leaving behind a cloud of dust. Pennsylvania. New Jersey. New York. Tomorrow would be another work day, regular and hard.

In the kitchen my father's mother looked tired, every one of her eighty-six years filling her eyes. She held onto the small table as she walked.

"Grandma, why don't you go to bed," I said.

"I reckon I will," she replied. I kissed her on the cheek. She stumbled and grabbed my shoulder to get her balance. "Is you gone get your daddy's car fixed?"

Her question jolted me. I hadn't given my father's Cadillac any thought since Uncle Cleat and I had left it at the mechanic's in Richmond. Soon I would be whipping around doing a "Detroit lean" out the window of George Moore's hog. Wouldn't he love to see that, I thought. "It's being fixed now, Grandma," I said.

"He sure did like that car," she mused almost to herself. "That boy loved pretty cars." She looked straight at me. "Don't bring it up the lane when you come. Hear?" I had to smile to myself. Grandma was loyal to the end. She stubbornly reasoned it was the machine at fault, and not her beloved son. I understood.

So I cleaned the kitchen, mourning my loss with each sweep of Grandma Mary's broom, each swipe of the battered dish cloth, and thought about this father whose entire possessions had fit neatly into the trunk of his yellow Cadillac, which now was mine.

I took my father's wheelchair back to D.C., even though Aunt Edith asked me if I wanted to give it to one of the old ladies in the neighborhood who was having a hard time getting around. I remember I said, "No, I want it," so fast and maybe so fiercely that Edith blinked and stepped away from me. Though why I wanted it, who knows. I put Daddy's chair in my basement and let it collect dust. Sometimes when I was washing clothes I'd look at it. The most I ever did was touch it occasionally.

In the months that followed, the fat insurance checks my father left me transformed my life-style, but at that moment I could feel his death reshaping my life, or at least the life I thought I was entitled to. There are gifts that only a father can give a daughter: his daily presence, his daily molding, his thick arm across thin girlish shoulder, his solemn declaration that she is beautiful and worthy. That her skin is radiant, the flare of her nostrils pretty. *Yeah, and Daddy's baby sure does have some big, flat feet, but that's all right. That's all right now. Come here, girl, and let Daddy see those tight, pretty curls, them kitchen curls.* I was all prepared to receive a daily ration of such gifts, albeit belatedly, but it was not to be. I would never serve beer and pretzels in the yard to Daddy and Tank. I would never have his company as I cleaned the dishes. He wouldn't see my daughter Maia's plays or her recitals. That was the way the cards had been dealt. I would go to my uncles, they wouldn't come to me. And the time for even those visits would later be eroded by obligations and miles. After April 1977 the old men in my life just plain thinned out.

For one thing, I got divorced and later remarried and moved far away to Los Angeles. After Grandma died, Uncle Johnny and Aunt Rena moved to Georgia near Aunt Rena's people. "You come see us," he told me before he left. "Don't forget; I'm your pop now." My Uncle Eddie finally sold his grocery store and moved from Philly to North Carolina, so I couldn't conveniently drop in at his market and chew the fat with him when I came to town to see Mom and Nana. Uncle Elijah died and I couldn't even go to his funeral, because my money was real funny that month. I sent flowers and called his wife, but what could I say? I should have been there.

My Marine uncle became a preacher. Uncle Sammy doesn't whoop and holler; his message is just plain good-sense gospel. He can even get scientific on you. When I hear his message I am thinking the whole time.

Uncle Norman and I still talk, but mostly on the telephone. My youngest uncle would call me up in hell, just to find out how I was getting treated. He is busy with his family and business. We don't see each other often.

The last time I saw Tank was a few weeks after the funeral, when he picked me up at the Greyhound bus station in Richmond and took me to get my father's car. Tank's skin is like a country night—no moon, no stars. You don't know what black is until you look in his face. Daddy always told me he wasn't much of a talker, and he's not, but he was just so nice and polite, sitting up in that big Lincoln, being my chauffeur. "Just tell me where you want to go," he said when I got into the car. We drove all over Richmond. Tank took me to where my father worked, to Mrs. Murphy's, everywhere.

Around two o'clock we pulled into McDonald's and he bought hamburgers, French fries and sodas for our lunch; the car was filled with the aroma of greasy food. We were both famished and we ate without talking at first. All you could hear was our lips smacking against our Big Macs. Al Green was singing, "Love will make a waaay . . ." on the radio. Tank looked at me and said, "Ole Be Be," as though astonished that little girls grow up and become women. He said my name the way older southerners are wont to, two distinct syllables. I love the sound. But it was weird, because as soon as he said my name like that, I caught sight of his wheelchair in the rearview mirror and at the same time thought about Maia, whom I'd left in D.C. with a girlfriend. I was still nursing her and I immediately felt pins and needles in my breasts, and when I looked at my blouse there were two huge wet milk rings. Tank looked, he looked away, then he looked again. Then he said, as if thinking aloud, "That's right. Moore's a grandaddy."

Tank's chair was very shiny in the mirror. His words hung between us real softly for a minute before I started up, which I'd sworn I wasn't going to do. I put my head on his shoulder and I just cried and cried and cried. Tears wouldn't stop. "George was right crazy about you, Be Be. Talked about you all the time. All the time," Tank said shyly. He offered up these words as the gift they were. I just nodded.

There have never been enough idle moments really to straighten out those tight, tight curls at the nape of my neck. Untangling a kitchen calls for a protracted, concentrated effort. You have to be serious. It is not a job for weak fingers on a summer's afternoon. Still, daydreaming fingers, even those caught up in tangles, reveal much.

It has proved to be true, what I felt looking into my father's satin-lined casket: my loss was more than his death, much more. Those men who used to entice me with their storytelling, yank my plaits, throw me quarters and tell me what a pretty girl I was are mostly beyond my reach now. But that's all right. When they were with me they were very much with me. My father took to his grave the short-sleeved, beer-swilling men of summer, big bellies, raucous laughter, pipe smoke and the aroma of cigars. My daddy is really gone and his vacant place is my cold, hard border. As always, my life is framed by his absence.

DICK'S GIRL

CHRISTINE O'HAGAN

THE LAST TIME I saw my father alive was on a broiling August day, inside a frigid hospital room he asked me not to leave. He was being treated again for his addictions, the illness caused by his excess.

The tan and white packs of Camels that he had smoked incessantly for years had practically disintegrated his lungs and what was left of his lungs had been tapped twice, while the Fleischmann's whiskey he swallowed by the quart was ruining the rest of him. He'd been in the hospital for weeks. His heart was failing and he'd been on a respirator: he was too weak to walk, and his feet so filled with fluid that he couldn't stand. The priest had been to see him every day of his stay and had given him the Last Rites three times.

I slept fitfully during those awful humid nights, thinking I was hearing the telephone. I kept waking at dawn, trapped in twisted, sweaty sheets, unable to quite believe that it was finally morning, that no ringing phone had shattered the black country night, that my husband, the boys, and I hadn't simply slept straight through the noise.

After my husband left for work every day, I sat at the kitchen table with my nightgown clinging to my skin, sipping tepid coffee, fortifying myself for the hundred-mile drive back and forth to the hospital with the boys. Bored with their comic books and games before we'd even reach the city line, they would squabble the whole rest of the way in the back seat.

One morning, while I showered, the children found the camera in the household rubble. Their pictures, developed nearly a year later, still shock me. Not only did it seem as though the boys would always be that round and that young, with that particular summer stretching on forever, but in the pictures, the house seemed run-down and neglected, as if it had been abandoned by us and taken over by careless strangers. The parched brown grass underneath the searing sun was long enough to swallow the boys up to their knees, and the gap-toothed neighborhood boys, grown up now, like mine, were sprawled all over the peeling front porch in a jumble of solitary sneakers and discarded T-shirts, baseball mitts, and long-nozzled water jugs. Popsicle sticks were stuck to the legs of their denim shorts. Somehow they managed to snap a picture of their little neighbor Joshua leaping for the ball, the glowing sun turning his dark hair amber, his white socks black on the soles, with his skinny legs jack-knifed behind him. But what I notice more are the white living room curtains in the bay window behind him, falling seedy and limp. Hanging from the porch, collapsed red impatiens straggle from crooked white pots trying so hard to do what was expected of them, like me, standing behind Joshua at the screen door, ghost-like in my short robe, with a pale and worried face, dreading, as I think back on it, the traffic on the Long Island Expressway and the maze of construction, and our shuddering old Ford, stalling in the soft asphalt like mud.

I didn't really think that he would die.

For I expected my father, who'd wanted to be a Marine and yet settled for the Air Force, a man partial to black leather jackets, guns, and Harley-Davidsons, to either live forever or just explode. Dying in a hospital bed had seemed to be all wrong for him. This death more suited to the sober-eyed fathers I'd met in my youth, not to someone who'd won a bet by driving a motorcycle into Duffy's Tavern in Flushing, from the front door straight through to the back.

I'd wanted a father who was sober and wise, not erratic, soaked in whiskey like mine. I'd wanted not a man whose greatest thrill in life was jumping out of airplanes, but a father who was a banker or a policeman or someone who worked on the railway express, a man who ushered at Mass in his gray-flannel suit, a born Catholic rather than a Protestant convert. I'd wanted a father who would know better than to leave me in the wrong parochial school classroom, a tiny weeping Hail Mary lost among the towering Our Fathers, the day of the Living Rosary Processional.

Although his job was normal enough—installing telephones throughout Manhattan—his approach was somewhat different: he threw his toolbox from one rooftop to the next and then leaped over the alleys rather than using the stairs. He carried a flashlight to hypnotize the rats when he worked in watery basements. After work he would disappear into the wee hours of the next day while his wife and children wailed and sobbed at the kitchen window, searching for him in the black streets, convinced that he was dead.

He said his idea of a good time was a day spent hunting deer or fishing; the rattlesnake he had shot and mounted when he was young was one of his prized possessions. But these were difficult pursuits for a country boy living in the city, especially one who spent so much of his time in the local gin mills. Other fathers seemed to make better use of their free time, joining the Knights of Columbus or the Holy Name Society, taking their families out for ice cream on a Saturday afternoon, or sponsoring one of the church dances my mother forced my father to attend in the new gray-flannel suit she had bought him (although he still wouldn't take off his boots). They would go with all the neighbors, the "fairy" men he'd laughed at, those same bankers and cops my mother encouraged him to play poker with on Friday nights although they had nothing in common, while my mother spent her free time planning the family outings he was forever disappearing from.

At the hospital, my father's room, at the end of the hall, was the first thing I would see when the elevator doors opened. As I stepped off and drew closer, I forced myself to focus on his belly, which seemed cheerfully rounded in his taut hospital gown—the result of his liver straining through his flesh. I wanted so much to be able to poke him with my finger, to have the sort of father I might tease about his appetite for spaghetti or chocolate cake.

Watching his middle made it easier for me to ignore the bundles of tubes and wires everywhere, and to avoid looking at his arms and legs, nearly skeletal despite the years of my mother's plump roasts and wonderful stews, despite the Irish pride she took in "running a fine table" from which he refused to eat. He preferred potato chips and saltines, or the dry boxes of brittle food their pantry was stocked with, to any of her home-cooked meals—although he ate hardly enough even of those things to keep a bird alive, despite my mother's wanting so desperately for him to live. On the rare occasion that he asked for ice cream, she would grab her purse and run off for a half-gallon of fudge ripple of which he barely would eat a tablespoon. The rest was stashed in the freezer to grow frost.

On his last day, my father wore a small green oxygen mask over his nose and mouth. He balanced himself on the edge of the bed when I walked through the doorway, his sticklike arms blackened by too many needles, too much drawn blood: his left arm had been strapped to a small wooden board that kept catching on the cotton blanket. His graying hair had been combed flat on his forehead by one of the younger nurses who told him, not mistakenly, that he looked like the actor Peter O'Toole.

He was alone, although I'd hoped so much that my mother would be there already, for I had never known him without a drink in his hand or a cloud of cigarette smoke around his face. Without that distraction, the vulnerability I saw in his huge hazel eyes, increasing with each visit, was nearly more than I could stand: how he'd lean forward when I came into the room, sensing that he had something to say and yet not wanting to hear it, finding it hard to look directly at him. He always seemed to be asking my tacit permission for— what?—he never said.

Struggling to breathe, he looked up at me as I hesitated at the threshold of the room and nodded. I felt momentarily confused by the slightness of his frame, his quivering lips, his shoulder blades so achingly thin they pierced the neckline of his gown. He was so frail that I could barely look at him, though I wanted to run over and hold him in my arms, as if he were one of my sons. I struggled with what to say, how to act. A major general sort of daughter in mime, I took a deep breath and strode to the chair next to his bed, examining somewhat imperiously his half-empty breakfast tray and his empty water glass. He stared at me, unable to speak, simply looking, continuously, openly, and finally I could only look back and shrug, closer to tears than I expected to be, telling myself that he had come out of heart failure before, had come home to wash down heart medicine with boiler-makers, placating my mother by swallowing his lozenge-shaped vitamin pills and his fizzling potassium drinks before his first beer of the day or his morning cigarette.

Hadn't I seen him leave for the OTB with the racing sheet in one hand and a pencil in the other when days before he'd seemed too sick to walk through the living room?

Besides, didn't everyone in the Heights laugh that he would bury us all?

And yet, if he wasn't the father I'd wanted, then I wasn't the daughter he'd expected—although I'd tried.

My father was an agile, dapper, and handsome man and I was heavy, taller than he was by the time I was 12, a bookish sort of girl who wore thick glasses and preferred to sit alone with a stack of books. This infuriated him; he wanted me to run through the streets with the other girls and "get some exercise." Yet the books I read helped me to figure him out. He reminded me of Rhett Butler in some ways, or one of Hemingway's men or even Jack Kerouac; in the movies, Paul Newman was so like him in "Hud." To please my father, I sometimes threw myself into the sidewalk's frenetic activity, sweating through a game of tag until he passed by and I could get away, wiping my face on my shirt all the way to the library.

I thought he might have wanted a son to do things with and although I had a baby brother, I tried to be a 1950s girl's idea of a boy, throwing myself on amusement park rides I was terrified of just because my father liked them, following him into the Atlantic Ocean, where the water was rough and far over my head.

(Years later, wearing a miniskirt, I climbed on the back of a perfect stranger's motorcycle just to see what he would say when he found out.)

That was long before we knew how handicapped my brother would be, that the future Marine my father had so hoped for was destined to spend his short life in a wheelchair.

I sat in the chair by my father's bed, staring at the speckled floor, trying not to listen to his gasps when he suddenly pulled the mask away from his face and balanced it on top of his head like a miner. He stared at his swollen purplish feet like a bashful young boy, mumbling softly that he had been a lousy father.

I was too stunned to answer him, but just then my mother appeared in the doorway, smiling broadly, carrying a shopping bag filled with goodies. She had met my father's young Korean doctor in the elevator, and he'd said my father was doing well, "holding his own" was how she put it, and now she finally felt secure enough, she said, to stay "but a minute" before running errands, shopping for groceries, going off to the bank.

She rushed past me and began to fuss with him, teasing him about his new hairstyle, helping him sit back against the pillows, covering his feet with a pair of warm socks she had pulled from her purse.

For nine years now, the scene stops there, with me watching my mother putting my father's socks on, tenderly holding his feet. I see it often at night, or sometimes when I'm scrubbing the tub, or when I can't sleep, wondering what would have happened if my mother hadn't appeared as suddenly as she did. On good days, I feel that I might have been unruffled enough, generous enough to fling my arms around his neck as I had wanted to do and forgive him for all of it, the drinking, the rages. On bad days, I'm not sure that I do forgive him, although I sometimes remember, in what seems like an old Waltons script, how he had patiently taught me to swim and, even more patiently, how to bait a hook. But those were two bright lights flashing throughout a long dark journey.

He was the most honest man I'd ever known; above everything else, he loved the truth. And he was right: he had been a pretty awful father.

For the longest time, I wished that I could have argued with him about that. I wished that I could remember some tender vague scene between us that would prove him wrong. But I still don't remember any and I don't think he would have, either: without a drink, he was morose and quiet and depressed. With one, he cried and laughed, raged and prayed out loud, then short-circuited, with some part of him worn thin and dangerous as frayed electrical cord. He threw furniture and fists and food, and then spent contrite Sunday mornings after church apologizing for things he never remembered doing.

When I was a young teen-ager, he sobbed one night for my lost babyhood, all wrapped up for him in the scent of Johnson's Baby Powder, and then he screamed that I was a tramp and hit me with his belt. Another time he cried at the memory of a fall I'd taken when a blonde toddler, and then punched me until the welts raised on my arms; afterward he tried to shove his overtime money into my purse. All of these things, except for the money, I'd stoically tried to accept, first indignantly and then finally forgiving him, running from the halting, blurry apologies that had seemed to shame us both.

I would devote myself once again to figuring him out, trying harder than ever to be good, riding back and forth to high school on the subway trying to forget his crazy accusations, trying so hard to be what he had wanted in a daughter, wondering how that blonde baby I had been had so utterly failed him.

On Friday nights, standing at the turnstile of the subway station, sent by my mother, I'd wait for my father to come home from work for what seems now to have been hours. Most of the time I'd show up either too early or too late, or near the wrong staircase, and usually I missed him in the throng of people. Looking for boots, I stared at weary nylon stockings, baggy at the knees, coming down the stairs, or vaguely-shredded cuffs on top of thin-soled scuffed loafers, waiting until the rush-hour crowd was down to the stragglers tweaking through the gate. Finally, I had to give up and leave, slowing for the walk up the street into the part of the search I hated most. I pressed my thick glasses to the front windows of the neighborhood bars until my lenses were scratched with grit, always shocked by the looks of pure hatred I got in return. The pairs of eyes looking at me out of the dark seemed shot with red, like the eyes of the very devil himself.

I don't think I would have been able to recognize my father if it weren't for the comma-shaped scar on the back of his head where he'd once been hit by a car: he was always smiling and so animated. He would laugh with Tiny (an old woman so small he'd have to pick her up and sit her on her stool), then stand with his arms around the shoulders of two disheveled men I'd have run from on the street. Once I watched him sing a song alongside a man missing his leg and the zipper in his slacks, a man with only a gaping hole where a zipper should have been; then he pretended to soft-shoe with the seedy parents of Ellen, one of the dirty girls at school who was shunned by the others, who smelled of unwashed hair and dirty laundry, who once had lent me a history book reeking of cigarette smoke.

Each time he saw me he waved for me to come in, but I was always frightened, always ready to run. Then, one of the women in the place always appeared in the doorway—bare-legged, her eyes struggling to adjust to the brightness of the outdoors—and grabbed for my hand. They all looked the same, these women, with red lipstick staining their yellow teeth, hairlines dyed along with their sparse hair, wrinkled clothes and whittled-looking high heels.

"Aren't you Dick's girl?" they'd ask, knowing that I was. Their hands were surprisingly soft and cool, mother's hands, wanting to be helpful, pulling me inside the blackness to where my father would steer me away from the bar and over to one of the tables. This is where the "ladies" sat, he said where I sat by myself, the people at the bar turning to stare at me now, in my light summer shorts. My father sent the bartender over with one Shirley Temple after another which I dutifully drank, until I had to pee so badly I could barely move and yet I was determined not to use the bathroom, as I'd have to pass the men staring at me, their groping hands resting on their knees. Instead, I pretended to listen to my father harmonize with some florid-faced man in a string tie who knew all the words to "My Wild Irish Rose."

In his hospital room, on my father's last day, I watched my mother pull a tin of butter cookies from her shopping bag and then a can of cold soda that she opened and poured into my father's bedside glass, the two of us watching her as intently as if she were consecrating wine at Mass, pressing the cup to his lips like a chalice.

Then she smoothed her hair and opened and closed her purse, her signal that she was ready to leave. But I anticipated it and was quicker, out of the chair and over to the door, petrified that my father and I might find ourselves alone again, that he, in his expression, might want to "square things."

That earlier moment was as close as I had wanted to be to an apology or even an explanation, and I was afraid to hear the rest of what he might have said: that he was a lousy father because he simply hadn't loved me.

"Don't leave," he pleaded, pulling at his mask with trembling fingers while I wanted to run down the stairs, out onto the street.

"The children. . . ." I said in a vague way, gesturing foolishly with my hand while he nodded miserably, while my mother waited out in the hall. "I'll come back," I promised, kissing his cheek damp with the oxygen's mist. I did just that later in the afternoon, but it was too late.

When my mother and I found him, he looked surprised: his dark eyebrows raised quizzically, no longer larger than life, no longer larger than death. Even he hadn't been ready for death, his ice-cream spoon halfway to his mouth, his ice-cream cup still frozen, his head lolled against his shoulder, his new hairdo a straggling mess.

We rang the buzzer. The nurses ushered us out and they called a code—code blue, just like in the movies. When it was over, they drew a curtain around his bed and asked me if I wanted to see him.

I shook my head no, for what was there left for me to say? I had tried so hard for so many years to know him and, at the end of his life, when the smoke had finally cleared and we faced each other, I simply ran away.

The next day, at the funeral home, I kissed Tiny's wrinkled cheek, although she was sobbing so hard her veil had slipped down over her eyes, and I shook hands with the assortment of rummy men who came holding Mass cards to pay their respects.

Even the man with the missing leg hobbled in, in pants that were stained but intact, and behind him, a friend of my late brother's, in dress blues, who'd come from camp somewhere or other, his Marines hat tucked underneath his arm.

Standing with my mother at the head of the casket, I greeted all of them like the lady my father had intended me to be, and at the last minute, before the casket was closed, I kissed his stony cheek, hearing the whispers all the way from the back row: "That's Dick's girl," they said, and I knew that they were right.

I was Dick's girl to the end.

JOHNNY'S GIRL
KIM RICH

A FRIEND OF MY parents once told me that I didn't
grow up—I was kicked up. I guess this is true. Orphan is not a word
I have ever used to describe myself but that's what I became with
the death of my father in August 1973. My mother had died a
year earlier.

It took months for the police to solve my father's murder and to
find his body. In the fall of '73 I entered tenth grade at East High
School in Anchorage. I attended pep rallies and struggled with
biology and algebra. I developed crushes on boys I'd see in the hall
and I attended after-school parties. More than anything, I tried to
pretend that my life had not changed.

I'd sit in my afternoon art class quietly drawing, listening to the
other girls gossip about who was going steady and the score of the
latest football game. I took refuge in their conversations and longed
to live on their streets and to be in their homes. I didn't want to face
what I knew some day I would have to deal with. I didn't want to

know that my father's body was stuffed in a sleeping bag and thrown into a shallow grave, a .45 caliber bullet shot through his heart.

The day I learned that my father was dead, I walked away from his world, severing all ties with my childhood. When my father's killers were tried, I avoided the courthouse and ignored the newspaper accounts, all of which echoed the same themes. My father—John F. "Johnny" Rich Jr., one of Anchorage's most notorious underworld figures—didn't return home one night from a visit to a local topless bar. I was 15 when my father was killed; he was 40.

Everyone knew my dad. Beginning in the late 1950s, he operated illegal gambling houses and occasionally ran prostitutes in Alaska's largest city. An only child, I was raised amid the denizens of Anchorage's nightlife—pimps, con men, gamblers, prostitutes, heroin addicts, and thieves. I spent most nights at home alone, staying close to the television for company while my father was out working the clubs.

I saw firsthand the ravages of "the life"; it broke my mother's spirit and triggered her collapse into insanity when I was just six years old. Cops and hoodlums would beat down the door to our home in the middle of the night. My father taught me to be tough and fearless. Yet I hated his life, and when I reached my teens we began to fight constantly about it.

"Why can't you be like other dads?" I'd yell at him. In a tired voice, he used to tell his friends, "You raise them just so they can grow up to hate you." That wasn't true. I loved my father, but for a long time there just wasn't much about him that I liked. We could hardly talk about anything without arguing and without my reminding him that I despised much of what he represented.

After his death, I finished my teen years living with the families of friends. I did okay. I graduated from a progressive, alternative high school geared toward high achievers. After high school I worked as a page in the state House of Representatives. I enrolled at the University of Alaska to study music, majoring in classical guitar. During my sophomore year, I switched my major to journalism. I competed on the varsity cross-country running and ski teams, and I graduated with honors in 1983. I married a handsome hometown boy and former U.S. Cross-Country Ski Team member. We bought a house in the mountains behind Anchorage and I began a career, working a year and a half in broadcast news before hiring on with the Pulitzer Prize-winning *Anchorage Daily News*, I lived a life that seemed to tally All-American—just the way I wanted it to be.

I wanted to put the first two decades of my life behind me and move on. I wanted to forget that my father had been murdered—a word I tried to avoid using when describing his death. "My father died when I was a teenager," was all I would say to anybody who asked. If pressed for more information, I'd slowly spill out the details. "He was shot," I'd say, hoping that would be the end of it. Usually however, I'd have to explain that no, he didn't die in a hunting accident. He was murdered. "Yeah, the killers were caught."

My mother? "She died of cancer." I always left out the part about her dying in a state mental institution. I didn't say much, in part because I didn't know much. I was purposefully vague also because I hated the way people would look at me once I began running through the whole story. I've always been too defensive; when I was younger, I mistook people's sympathy for pity, and I wanted none of the latter. I'd always end these conversations about my history and the past by saying, "I'm fine." Indeed, I was: determinedly so.

As I grew older, though, I began to feel as if something was missing from my life, even from my identity. I had no sense of belonging or personal history. In the place of childhood memories and connections was a void, and as I moved into my mid-twenties, it widened and deepened. I was haunted by many things: my father's lifestyle, his death, my mother's illness. I now look at early photos of my parents and I am reminded of when I first began to wonder what went wrong. I was a freshman in college when my mother's two sisters sent me a couple of picture albums that my mother had kept and which my aunts had been caretaking, intending to pass them along to me once I was grown.

The first time I looked at the photographs I saw my father not only as I remembered him but how he must have looked to my mother when she fell in love with him.

A casting agent could have named my father—he was of medium build, lithe and handsome, with dark, curly hair that he combed back in neat waves. He wore custom-tailored silk suits and smoked Lucky Strikes. To my mother, Frances Ann Chiaravalle, a small-town Catholic girl, he seemed urbane, sophisticated, and worldly. And there were so many compelling mysteries about him, not the least of which was a tattoo—his Social Security number—engraved on his left bicep.

When they met my mother had taken to enhancing a beauty mark on her left cheek, in the style of Marilyn Monroe, and she began to call herself "Ginger." With her pronounced cheekbones and heart-shaped lips painted cherry red, my mother was exquisite. She dressed in skintight pedal pushers and cashmere sweaters, a true fifties beauty.

My parents, who met in Los Angeles in 1956, seemed to be custom-made for each other, both with pasts that were better forgotten. Soon after I was born in 1958 they moved to Anchorage, seeking their fortune before Alaska became a state and its frontier spirit was tamed. My father worked as a professional gambler; my mother, a stripper and "B-girl"—a high-priced cocktail waitress who sold drinks on commission. For a few short years they lived their own version of the American Dream, buying a new home and new cars: a white Cadillac convertible for him; a cherry-red Corvair for her. But soon their dream began to slip away, and by the time I entered first grade, my mother was institutionalized for schizophrenia and my father continued to live his life on the edge of the law. Despite this, he successfully fought the courts for custody of me.

Growing up, it was always just my father and I. He seemed to have no other family members—there were no calls from grandparents, uncles, or aunts. My father's background was a mystery to me, and this mystery only grew the day, not long after his death, when his accountant mentioned that Rich was probably not even his real last name. I wasn't sure what to make of this news. The accountant couldn't tell me what my father's real name might have been, only that he remembered my father once mentioning that he had another name.

I tucked this new piece of the puzzle in the back of my mind, deciding that someday I would try to find out if this was true, whether it fit into the larger picture. Not long after I graduated from college I began to hunt for the answers and gradually to put the pieces together.

I started my search in fits and starts. As a cub reporter, I happened onto a wire service story about unclaimed bank accounts, leading me to wonder what had happened to my father's accounts after his death. Later, as a court reporter with the *Daily News*, I looked up his criminal record, copying each case number onto a list that filled two sides of a sheet of legal paper.

The research into my father's banking practices merely reinforced for me his criminal mystique. I learned that he rarely kept personal bank accounts, preferring to work with cash or opening accounts under corporate identities. Both strategies helped him elude any official inquiries into his finances, such as subpoenas from the

Internal Revenue Service or warrant-wielding creditors with court judgments that granted them access to my father's assets.

All it took was a cursory glance at his court record and a number of revelations came to light, not the least of which was that my father's police and court record, however lengthy, was comprised only of misdemeanor offenses, mostly gambling. There were no robberies, no assaults, and nothing more criminally serious than shouting obscenities at police officers (at one time this was against the law in Alaska). I quickly came to realize that my father wasn't the criminal I might have believed him to be when I was a teenager.

I was relieved, yet there was still much I did not know. But at the time I was too busy, and likely not emotionally ready, to dig any deeper. Even then I sensed that my search would be a process of things working themselves from the inside out. I would do and learn only that which I was somehow prepared to take on.

It wasn't until I was twenty-seven and working on a feature story about my father for the *Daily News* that my research began in earnest. The story was intended to commemorate the tenth anniversary of the completion of the trans-Alaska pipeline. I was to write about my father and his role in Anchorage's underworld around the time pipeline construction began.

I knew from my father's driver's license application that he was from Connecticut. I tried to find a birth certificate but was unsuccessful, and with little else to go on, a records clerk in Hartford said she couldn't help me. I'd hit a dead end and in frustration I gave up. I had what I needed for the scope of my newspaper story and my deadline required that I move on.

Two years later I resumed my quest when I began a book based upon the newspaper story. I still had little information when I telephoned a genealogical society to enlist their help. I can still remember the way the woman who headed the society sighed when I told her my situation. "My father was from Connecticut," I said, or so I thought. "His name was John Rich, but then he might have had another name. He said he was born in 1930, but that could be false too," I pointed out. The only other information I had were four names my mother had penciled into a family tree on a page in my baby book. Under the heading of my father's father she'd written: "John F. Rich Sr."; his mother was named "Helen Fickett"; and my great-grandparents were named "Leonard and Rose Rich."

That phone call was the beginning of a search that would take the better part of four years to complete. I got to know records clerks in three states. Genealogical researchers helped me scan city directories and census records dating back to 1900, seeking traces of his family. Everyone had believed my father to be Jewish and so I joined a synagogue to make contact with my spiritual roots. I even took Hebrew lessons. I called complete strangers and said, "I think you may be my grandfather."

I tracked down my father's friends and business associates—men who once wielded great power in Anchorage's underworld but had long since retired. I spoke with the policemen who busted him; the lawyers who defended him. I reviewed thousands of pages of FBI, court, and police documents on my father's activities.

I contacted dozens of state, federal, and private child welfare agencies, and mailed at least 100 inquiry letters. To my surprise, perfect strangers went out of their way to look for records, search for clues, find anything they could that might lead me to find out who my father was as a child. I wanted to know where he was born; where he'd grown up; what baseball fields he had once played on; where he had gone to school; what did he look like? I knew intuitively that if I could know my father as a boy, I might begin to understand him as a man.

What I would eventually learn was as shocking as it was sad. My father was born illegitimate and was raised in foster homes and state institutions. He was not Jewish, yet for reasons that still remain a mystery, he told some people that he was. He never talked about his family because he never really had one. I understood then why he was determined, despite his life-style, to be a father to me, and this realization deepened my love for him.

Once I knew where my father had come from and what his own childhood had been like, I felt ready to face the facts about his death. The answers now fill several filing cabinets in my office. Scores of manila folders hold the bits and pieces of my father's murder. I had gotten them from the courthouse when the clerks were cleaning out an old evidence vault. A notice was posted but nobody lay claim to the files, which were nearly twenty years old.

At the front of one court file, a lengthy index describes the contents—"Power of Attorney," "White Envelope," "Brown Envelope," "Latent Fingerprints," ".45 Cal Pistol (photo of)," "Photos of Cabin." Everything is stamped with yellow and white stickers—"Plaintiff's Exhibit 10, 74–1734 Cr," "State's Exhibit 22, 74–1734 Cr"—and wrapped in clear plastic or stapled neatly to sheets of crisp, white paper.

The envelope with the handwritten label State v. Ladd is another matter. That folder contains plastic bags made brittle by time and sealed with the red tags used by the troopers to describe the contents. One bag holds locks of my father's hair, others contain scrapings from the spot where he died, fragments of linoleum and wood, a twist-off beer cap, loose cigarette tobacco. The last holds one of the slugs that killed him.

While I was trying to crack the mystery of my father's life, I also began tracking my mother's story. Though I was acquainted with her family they were reluctant to provide much information on how she became ill. I contacted half a dozen hospitals and mental institutions, talking with her doctors, caretakers, and old friends, seeking clues to who she'd been before the shock treatments and straitjackets. She had had her first serious breakdown at age 19 and was institutionalized off and on for a year, often subjected to weeks of terrifying shock treatments. This would haunt her all of her life. During her marriage to my father, she was in the midst of a ten-year period of relative good health, and during this time she was considered good company, fun to be around, and a kind and generous friend. In the end, hers was no failure of will or personal fortitude, as I had once believed, but that of biology.

For a long time during my research I didn't feel a thing. I was so busy digging for information that I never gave much thought to the emotional consequences. The pace was exhilarating—I was learning new things every day. I felt more like a reporter on the trail of a hot story than a daughter who simply wanted to remember and understand her parents.

Somewhere along the way, about a year into my search, that all changed. I began to feel an enormous sense of loss. But what was it that was gone? All I knew was that the more I learned, the more I felt that something inside of me was shifting, being altered. Maybe forever. My marriage eventually ended for reasons that will never be easy to articulate. In part, we simply grew distant and like many couples we took each other for granted. Though we separated a year before I began my search into my past, I believe it was in part due to the process of my turning inward.

About a year into my book research I began to feel a deep sorrow. Months would pass and I felt vulnerable in a way I never had before. I felt cheated, envious of all around me who had families as if noticing for the first time that my parents were gone. Mostly I felt lonely and overcome by an irreconcilable grief. The confidence that had gotten me through all the years of my life seemed shattered and I wondered if I would ever get it back again. The darkest part of this period of my life lasted about a year.

During the worst of it, even daily life became difficult: the smallest disappointments seemed unbearable, minor defeats appeared insurmountable, and at times simply moving forward seemed pointless. Some of my closest friends weren't sure they even knew me. Seemingly gone was the relentless optimism, the chirpy and spunky nature that had endeared me to even the most hard-bitten of newsroom editors. I've always had a wide circle of friends and many offered emotional and even financial support while I worked on the book. Some didn't notice the changes in me, though, and were surprised to hear me talk about such feelings. But I felt as if I'd been suddenly and grievously crippled and was moving through life with an emotional limp. I began to question whether the pain would end. I wasn't sure I even knew where it was coming from. It was then I realized that I had never felt any pain over the loss of either of my parents. *Survive, look forward, don't look back.* I'd only postponed it.

"I'm not so sure that this whole business of dredging up my childhood has been such a good idea," I told my friend Averil Lerman over the phone one night. "I feel lost."

Averil is a wise, compassionate woman whom I have always turned to during such moments. I trust Averil. It was she who looked at the photographs in my mother's albums and helped me see my parents as I had not seen them before: as people, not just parents. It was because of her insights that I went to her whenever I felt overwhelmed, and I'll always remember our conversation that night.

"I know too much," I told her. "Every time something goes wrong now, it all seems to tap into the past. All the disappointments come tumbling down. I am tired of wading through it all and I'm not sure it's been worth it."

Averil insisted then, as she always does, that it was the only way. "You've gained everything," she said. "You're a dragon-slayer now."

"Yes, but at what cost?" I asked.

Then Averil offered an answer I've never forgotten.

"There is no way past, but through."

She was right. I always knew, deep inside, that I would someday have to go back and come to terms with my past. After my father's death, even at age 15, I had decided that I would write about him as a way to remember him. Maybe that was what all my training in journalism had been about. But only as an adult could I understand the choices he made and the circumstances that had shaped his life. Nothing I learned—no fact, no anecdote, no criminal record— seemed so terrible or mysterious that it could not be examined and embraced. I came to understand his values and to see that he was more honest than was ever obvious, more generous than imagined, and, most important, in more pain than he had ever shown. I learned to forgive him for his explosive temper, his absences at night, his inability to forge a lasting relationship with any woman after my mother, and his perfectionism when it came to me. It was a rarely spoken but everpresent expectation that I would never fail, perhaps because he felt he had done so far too many times: when my mother grew ill, when his straight jobs went bankrupt, and when, as a teen, I found him so dislikable.

My look back helped me at times to hate him, to love him, and to grieve his loss, but ultimately to know myself. To understand my father's strengths, weaknesses, and vulnerabilities is to know my own. I now have a valuable sense of roots that my father never had, and I feel some sense of triumph to have broken a cycle that might have continued.

People say I look just like him and there was a time when I'd brush aside this suggestion. Now when I look into a mirror and pull my hair back, I see his face staring back at me and it no longer troubles me.

I DON'T BELIEVE
IN GHOSTS

JULIA BANKS

I WAS EIGHT WHEN he left, two days into nineteen
when he died. The college students around me were as awkward and
uncertain as I was, and the situation seemed to require more grace
and honesty than we had. They offered me a belated chocolate
birthday cake and leftover pizza. I felt like I should talk about him, so
that first evening I cried with these people I barely knew while they
watched, patient and distant. I sat on the top bunk in a cinderblock
room. Three people from down the hall gazed up at me and learned
about being supportive. My roommate pointed out that I didn't really
know my father so it didn't really matter that he was dead. After that
night, no one mentioned him.

My family decided to have a memorial service the following
summer, six months away. A funeral was out of the question; my
father had put too much time and distance between himself and
anyone else who might care enough to attend a real funeral. Other

families rally after a death. We put it off and opted for a summer funeral to get maximum attendance. Who are those people who make last-minute plane reservations, drop or postpone the normal activities of life, for someone who has gone? Too difficult, too expensive, we decided. When my father died, I didn't miss a single class, or turn in any late papers.

In Louisville, my sister arranged for a service the day after he died. Three people came, two church ladies and her. That day, I went to a rehearsal room and played scraps of hymns on a crooked upright piano. I remembered the day years ago when our third guinea pig died. My mom and two of my sisters buried him in the yard while I stayed upstairs and played a funeral march, the same five or six bars, over and over.

So through the rest of that winter I trudged back and forth to class. I stayed quiet, studious, and felt distant from all the faces around me.

My mother says time will heal all wounds. She means it to be reassuring. She sometimes adds, "Time wounds all heels." I think: Does she mean my father? She also says that salty tears help heal wounds. I'm not so sure. I've been crying about this for a long time, but I don't feel any better.

My father first left when I was eight, on a day that seemed to be more about moving than about leaving. We borrowed a red dolly to cart boxes from our house to an apartment. My father helped us move. I remember him in the yard: tall, in blue jeans and blue work shirt, wheeling that red dolly across the dirty gravel yard, the wheels clanking. That sound can remind me of him, and I see his tall frame with the metal cart in the yard. He made some silly kid's joke to me about the cart, "dolly," a girl's name.

I rode my bike away to play with friends. When it was time to go home, I went to our old house. It was completely empty now, quiet. I wandered around, opening cupboards, closets, and drawers, looking for something I recognized. Nothing had been left behind. I went through the basement and the garage, wondering at the stillness. I went out into the yard and got back on my bike. I found my way to the new apartment by a few landmarks: candy store, stucco house, lilac bush. When I got back to the apartment, my father had gone, driven away in our pale green Impala. My mother said, "Your father said to say good-bye to you." Later, the owner of the red dolly called to ask about its return. My father had driven to Texas in the pale green Impala with the red dolly.

It was a gradual revealing of facts: your father is sick; it's something with his liver, his lungs; your father is very sick. He probably spent a couple of years dying before I was really aware of it. I saw two images of him after he left. One was a pencil sketch of his face in profile. It was a large drawing kept between the pages of a large book on the bookshelf. I rediscovered it several times. It was always something of a shock, the flip of a page and then the image flying out at me like an irrepressible memory. The other, stored similarly, was a photograph of him taken beside the green pickup truck he bought in Texas. Both pictures were difficult to find, and only seemed to surface when I wasn't thinking about finding them. I don't know where they are now, although I could find out.

If I concentrate I can remember his voice. It was rich, not deep, careful and slow, cynically humorous. It must have brought people toward him. He called me jay bird, blue jay, brown eyes, sharp eyes. But I can't remember any specific thing he ever said to me; I can't recall a conversation or a phrase. I remember walking with him down the sidewalk, holding his hand. We were on our way to buy a new doll to replace one the neighbor's dog had chewed up. I skipped, feeling myself smile, full of kid-happiness for being alone with my father, on our way to buy me a doll. He laughed and skipped, too. I stopped, suddenly embarrassed. He stopped when I did, then I began again and so did he.

At times I would lie in bed at night, snug under the covers, and hear my father walking up the stairs, bumping steps or sometimes brushing against the wall. It was the last of the household's settling-down noises. I would hear him and feel safe; I knew I was loved and cared for, and I knew my family would always be together.

I can recall my parent's reconciliations but no arguments. My clearest memory is an image of them standing embraced, framed in the bathroom door. The faucet is running. They are both tall, my mother tall enough to rest her chin on my father's shoulder. It was a static moment of forgiveness; now I remember the scene and see failure rising like steam from the bath.

After the divorce, my mother explained things to me. I had come home late from school one day, wearing my brownie scout uniform. My sisters had already eaten dinner and gone outside, and my mother and I were alone in the apartment. I told her I wanted to go live with my dad; I had been planning it for a long time. She told me then that he was an alcoholic. "I thought you knew," she said. "Why do you think we got divorced?" I didn't know. She told me how he stumbled drunk up the stairs many nights. The next thing I remember, we are in the bathroom. Maybe she is about to run me a bath, because she is sitting on the edge of the bathtub. I am draped on her lap facing her, my legs over the side. I see this scene from outside, above it. The body in the brown outfit is limp, crying.

Years later, standing, sorting things from my mother's drawer, we come upon a box of jewelry. A tiny bent garnet ring, a silver and turquoise cross on a necklace. My mother holds up the silver cross, also slightly bent and tarnished. "We could repair this; it's from your father." I knew that. A headache built behind my eyes. I didn't want to cry. I asked why he gave jewelry to me and not to her, but I really didn't want to hear an answer. I already knew that she lost her wedding ring at the beach when I was a baby. I also knew that he never bought her another one.

I am the observer, the listener. I learned how to keep myself still until I absorbed everything. Afterward, I could think about the information, examine it when I was alone. I imagined myself holding all of this painful knowledge inside, where I could smother it, along with my confusion. I meant my calmness to signify strength, an ability to deal with anything that came. Later, I would cry. Uncertainty and longing came out at night. I would turn my pillow over to the dry side and wake up feeling fine.

I threw away his letters at some point, sometime after I knew he was sick, but before he died. I remember thinking I didn't need them. I also refused to talk to him when he called. The telephone line only emphasized the distance, and did not ease my sadness. One Saturday morning I pretended to be asleep to avoid my turn on the phone with him. I can't remember what we said to each other when we did talk or what the letters contained.

When my father got sick he drove from Houston to Louisville. Painkillers were his only medication; and nothing else could help him. I pictured him driving recklessly, swallowing pills, swiping guard rails and bridge walls. He drove to a veteran's hospital near where my oldest sister lived. Sometimes I ask her about his last days, but not very often. He didn't acknowledge his impending death; he didn't say, "I'm afraid." He didn't even say good-bye to her or to anyone else. My mother asked her these same questions.

I used to imagine myself going to visit him in Louisville before he died. I thought about how I could justify asking my mom for the money, for the time off from school. I saw myself at eighteen, stepping off an airplane, toward a taxi that would take me to the hospital. I couldn't imagine what would happen next.

It never seemed strange to me that he died so far away from anything or anyone. There must have been some silence, some blankness in his heart. His stumbling, his blurring himself in alcohol, his physical distance—those were his choices. He could not have loved me and left.

I do not believe in ghosts but I try not to think about them anyway. On a sleepless, breathless, sweltering night I begin to think of my father. What would he say to me if he were here? I place him in scenes from my life, I hear phrases, ". . . proud of you. . . ." "come here, jaybird." But nothing about this seems real. I don't really want him here anyway. Not the way he was.

I also imagine him seeing me vomiting rum into a gutter, or lighting a cigarette. No words accompany these daydreams. My father doesn't say anything to me, no matter what I do.

When I look in the mirror or at old photographs of him, I recognize the forehead, eyebrows, brown eyes, wide sideways smile. I try to tell my mother I don't want anything different from what I have. I don't wish anymore that I tried to see him, and I no longer spend time wishing he could see me now. Not much time, anyway.

I suppose I must find my father, and find out what these memories and feelings mean to me. There is no new information available; the facts won't change. If I rearrange and reinterpret, what difference will that make? Whenever I think about any of this I encounter confusion and anger, and always end up crying. I'd rather leave all of this where it lies, at the bottom of my heart.

ARCHAEOLOGY

JOAN ALLISON SHIEL

I HAVE TO ADMIT that I never felt grown-up around my father. In the magic world of childhood he was a king—all wise, all-powerful—and I was the little daughter (not a princess) who needed his guidance and protection. We never really left that enchanted world, even when I moved away from home and established my own independent life. For reasons that are undoubtedly complex, we played out our years together in a kind of time-warp theater, with my father cast as the adult and me as the child. We never became peers in a grown-up world beyond the stage. When I grew older, I had an awareness of my role-playing and its cost—maintenance of distance from my father and the concealment of my true self. Only with his death when I was 55 years old did I begin to understand that my father, too, had been playing a part. Behind the role had been a flesh-and-blood human being, unique and irreplaceable, a man now gone for whom I needed to search and find so I could say good-bye.

On the day my father died the curtain fell. I walked off the stage and emerged from the theater as a middle-aged woman. For the first time I felt like my father's peer. I assumed responsibilities—to my mother, to other family members, and to his memory. These duties ranged from the sheerly practical to the spiritual and psychological. They offered certain rewards, like the pleasures of being competent, effective, and useful. Freed from a child's self-centered perspective I found it possible to understand that only part of his life involved being my father. The child had feared to ask too many questions; the woman was filled with curiosity. I needed to discover more about my father, to measure my losses so I could complete the grieving process and move on with my life.

*****

The attic of the house where my father lived and died, and where I grew up, over the years had become his private place. It was a sort of miniature library/museum where he worked and stored his various collections. My mother rarely ventured up there. The same was true for me. It was filled with his spirit and would, I felt, contain important clues to the man. So I decided to become an archaeologist, unearthing artifacts, examining the potsherds: an historian, piecing it all together to find new meanings.

In the attic I feel close to my father when I sit at the old black walnut dining table he used as a desk. Although strongly built, the table is not what it once was; the drop leaves need reinforcement and the claw-footed center pedestal is no longer sturdy. It belonged to his grandparents, and accompanied my father through his 87 years of life. It was a workbench in his boyhood, a place to do homework during school and college days, and finally, like a faithful dog, still at his side in old age.

Other antiques reside in the attic: an Edison phonograph with cylinders from the early 1900s, a child's cradle, a rocker, clocks, and an old Melodian, moved up here from the living room downstairs. I have vivid memories of my father sitting at the Melodian, pumping like mad and belting out "Abide with Me." Maps and prints and photographs hand in the stairwell and on the vertical walls. Shelves, both open and glass-fronted, of different heights and depths, occupy every feasible spot.

My father was an enthusiastic collector, and his shelves contain the eclectic accumulation of a lifetime—books, pamphlets, newspapers, maps, manuscripts, photographs, prints, letters, albums, documents, stamps—an almost endless proliferation of paper. When I first entered the attic after my father's death, it seemed topsy-turvy, perhaps because of material piled on the floor, protective book jackets fashioned from old Christmas wrappings, and the shabby envelopes and folders he used to stash clippings and pamphlets. After I started to work in the attic I found that all the collected items had been classified, marked, and assigned shelf-space by category. Cross-referenced card files and lists turned up. This organization, well disguised behind the apparent disorder, added new depth to memories of my father's disappearances during social occasions. He would often slip away, only to return triumphantly with a book, map, or photograph pertaining to the conversation at hand or a guest's special interest. Now I know that he wanted to amaze and please people, but kept secret the hard work and thought that made this possible. I recognize that I too have always had a desire to make things look easy, and that it is more than coincidental that my father and I share this trait.

*****

When I look in the mirror I see my mother's cheekbones and brown eyes, my father's chin and dark hair, but have come to feel part of a more complicated gene pool. Unlike either of my parents, I have fair freckled skin, inherited from the red-headed man who was my father's father, dead long before I was born. I had never even seen his picture. When I opened the albums and shoe boxes of photographs stored away on the attic shelves, I found my grandfather's photograph in a pictorial family archive stretching back almost 150 years, well into the 19th century. In some way I felt substantiated, and these photographs haunted me. I spread them out on the walnut table forming a sort of genealogical jigsaw puzzle as I identified individuals by name and placed them within the family history. I scrutinized their never-before-seen faces for my own physical traits. Based on their clothes and hairstyles and attitudes, as well as their faces, I formed impressions about these individuals. In an imaginary world of my creation they came to life. Among the best-looking were the baby who grew up to become my father, and his mother, a handsome brunette with an elaborate Victorian hairdo and large eyes I remember as being blue. A formal baby picture shows my father at about two years of age, looking slightly worried but alert and beautiful, greatly resembling his mother with long dark curls, and huge eyes. It tickled me to look at this baby face and detect the man I had known. But it took effort to reconcile the vivid young woman in the studio portrait with the old grandmother I knew, and to accommodate the idea that one of her pretty little daughters had become the sick old woman I visited in a nursing home. I was older than the people in the photographs, yet most of them were dead and gone. It was a disorienting new perspective. These people meant something to my father. Many were identified in his handwriting as "Aunt Ellie" or "Uncle George." I realized that my father probably looked at these photographs with thoughts and feelings similar to my own. He too may have felt haunted by them, disoriented by the passage of time, and like me, thought about mortality and the loss of a once familiar world.

At first overwhelmed, perceiving myself as an intruder, I gradually became more comfortable in the attic; over a period of years, I lived with my father's collections and became sensitive to his idiosyncracies and preferences. I skimmed through periodicals and news clippings, browsed through books, reading some of them, particularly enjoying his coments in the margins and on scrap paper inserts. Most revealing were his own writings, his correspondence and drafts for books and magazine articles. Pages of his introspective musings about more personal subjects filled many folders and notebooks. When my mother and I decided to give most of my father's collections to appropriate libraries and an historical society, I began to prepare the material for donation by designing book plates, computerizing the card files, removing the tattered dust jackets, and affixing proper labels. I am happy that I could collaborate with my father in this way, but it was a slow and emotional process that included so much reflecting and remembering. I detoured often down dim side roads in my own past, confronting many ghosts. Nearly forgotten memories of my father emerged with deeper significance. My rewards were the discovery of an imperfect yet immensely warm and loving man whose loss I was able to acknowledge, along with a new sense of my own emotional capacities as I recognized that my work in the attic has been a labor of love.

*****

It was easy to like my father in the role he played. He was an old-time kind of guy, the kind "they don't make 'em like anymore," filled with 19th-century virtues such as self-reliance, honesty, and optimism. Something about him said "farmer" although he was an electrical engineer by profession. He wore the Puritan work ethic becomingly and it didn't seem to interfere with his sense of humor. My father's interests were wide-ranging and his head was filled with an amazing amount of information. He could converse intelligently about Eskimos or Seth Thomas clocks. He could construct a burglar alarm system or rebuild the fish pond. Yankee know-how was his forte and he could jerry-rig with the best. He could grow anything and never stopped experimenting with his garden. My father was a Quaker, having joined the Society of Friends in mid-life. (I was pleased when a Quaker acquaintance said that to know him was to feel certain that Quakers were alive and well on Long Island.) He was an authority on local history, the focus of his largest collection of books and documents. The man I've come to know can still be described in these words, but now there is another dimension which adds depth and substance, making it possible for me to feel compassion and identify with him, rather than merely appreciate an attractive performance.

He had been sentimental, indiscriminately accumulating mementos of those he loved as if wastebaskets hadn't been invented. I was embarrassed, amused, and sad to unearth my poorly-written sixth grade book reports, inept high school drawings of movie star crushes, snobby letters from college asking for money. How I had bewildered my father with low grades, rebellious behavior, arguments with my mother, and—later on—a divorce. He had not felt much pride in me during those years of my growing up. I had been angry and let down by his unwillingness to help me when I almost failed chemistry or was unsure of myself socially. Whenever life threw me a curve he kept himself at a very, very safe distance. I wish he had been there for me with advice, comfort, or constructive criticism, but maybe all-wise kings can't get too close if they don't have all the answers themselves.

I am newly aware that my father's interests—gardening, reading, writing, the study of history—tended toward the solitary, and may have been a form of escapism. Now it also seems clear to me that his greatest escape came from withdrawing into the lost world of his happy childhood. It seems more than coincidental that much of what he chose to collect was related to those early years. Perhaps he, like me, had trouble feeling grown-up, and found himself more comfortable in the safe and enchanted realm of the past. I realized that my father and I had more in common than I'd ever imagined. These insights enabled me to look at aspects of his behavior that had always confused and disturbed me and, as the pieces came together, I began to perceive a bigger picture.

During his lifetime I was aware that while my father often chose to stand apart, keeping his feelings private, his warm nature and lively intellectual curiosity about the world drew him toward people and activities. On the one hand he was emotionally introverted; he avoided debts and was cautious about commitments of any sort. He paid cash for almost everything, even his cars, and freely proclaimed that he was not a "joiner." On the other hand, he participated fully, even joyously, in the organizations he did join—for example, the Friends Meeting. He generously gave time, effort, and money to many individuals.

I now believe that this inner conflict resulted from his fear of being overwhelmed by obligations and trapped by his own feelings. The carefully preserved documents pertaining to the sudden untimely death of his father helped me to better understand these conflicts. My father, barely 16, was pushed prematurely into adult responsibilities when he was obliged to leave school and get a job to support his mother and two sisters. Surely he felt overwhelmed by these grown-up responsibilities. Reading his mother's letters telling him he was now "the man in the family" and pleading that he "just do the right thing; just do your part" made me sense the pressure he must have felt. He was still writing about the painful events of those years shortly before his death. I find it easy now to see why he often longed for the carefree years of childhood.

In the attic I came to appreciate my father's capacity for change and growth. From his writings I know he worked at self-improvement, frequently reflecting on his own values and character traits. Just before he died he was asking, "What is happiness?" and considering "hubris" as a possible problem that he must overcome.

Throughout my childhood, I remember that my father was suspicious of strangers, often treating them with rude indifference. For many years he wouldn't cope with unpleasantness or with people he disliked. He just withdrew in silence, escaping as soon as possible to his garden or attic. Because of this somewhat antisocial behavior, there were people who actually were afraid of him. The fact that he changed much over the years was proven to me at his memorial service. A man I didn't know stepped forward to say that he had been apprehensive about being the first black person to move into the white middle-class community in which my parents lived . . . until my father strolled by with his dog, struck up a conversation, and began a neighborly friendship based on a mutual interest in gardening. This man, who had moved away from that area years ago, still had known my father well enough to take a morning off from work and drive miles to attend the service.

I have found that the attic reflects a man who wanted to share his interests and ideas, not an introvert who avoided intimacy. He left behind a paper trail leading to his inner thoughts and feelings, complete with warts. My father had time to cover his tracks, but instead he left his history there as if he hoped it would be found and read.

*****

After Charles Lindbergh died, it was said that his wife Anne Morrow Lindbergh commented that a man's life is like a tree: you see that the tree has grown high, but only when it falls in death do you realize its true height. Perhaps meanings and true measures can come only with endings. The man I discovered in the attic was vulnerable and more complicated than the invincible king of my childhood. I have concluded that my father experienced a full range of emotions: from sorrow, frustration, and anger to joy, fulfillment, and love. It is clear that my father found life rich and interesting, and because of that I believe he was a happy man.

The unique individual who was my father is gone forever and I will always miss him. I've said good-bye but now there is an abundance of meaningful memories to comfort me. I've also said good-bye to childhood, but through remembrance, still have access to that magical world where I once was a little girl who thought her Daddy could do anything. I don't try to live there anymore but I sometimes enjoy a visit, as my father did. I cherish this bond between us. In the final words of *The House at Pooh Corner*, A. A. Milne captures these feelings perfectly; Christopher Robin says good-bye to his beloved Winnie-the-Pooh, and symbolically, bids farewell to his childhood: ". . . wherever they go, and whatever happens to them on the way, in that enchanted place on the top of the forest, a little boy and his Bear will always be playing."

How paradoxical role-playing is. It keeps people apart and yet draws them together. Roles preclude intimacy but also help to keep the show on the road. Like tent poles, the parts we play hold up the family structure, providing its members with shelter from the cold. That, finally, was the way of my family, especially in the last years. I am happy we observed the formalities, celebrating birthdays and holidays together. I am glad we found common ground through shared books, discussions about politics, excursions, and television watching. It is true we kept things light and non-intimate, but I'm grateful for the warmth of these memories.

It was liberating to discover that my father was not the all-wise king of my childhood but instead was a real person who didn't always feel grown-up or all-wise. Having learned this, I was able to relinquish some of the unidentified grievances I'd been carrying for years. It was healing to do away with the misconception that I had an all-powerful father who owed his daughter a life where everything came easily, where there is only success, never grief, disappointment, or any of the challenges of life.

It feels good to acknowledge the human imperfection of real people, myself very much included, and to know that imperfect love is still love. I suppose this means I am grown up.

THE STEEPEST RIDGES
ON A MOUNTAIN

MARY MARTIN NIEPOLD

NOT LONG AGO I watched the film, *To Kill a Mocking-bird*, and remembered that when it first came out thirty years ago, I was stunned by the similarities between some of the characters and my family. I instantly identified with Scout, the little girl growing up in a small Southern town, and I saw my Daddy in Atticus, Scout's father, who is a lawyer.

My father was very much like Atticus. Besides being a lawyer, his thoughtful personality seemed to get even quieter when he was delivering some lesson. I looked up to my Daddy, I think, like many little girls look up to their fathers. He was gregarious and playful most of the time when I was a very young child, but by the time I was six, he was pulled deeper into the isolated corners of alcoholism. This was during the late forties, and because of his illness my mother had to start going to work every day. My brother and I scrambled in the confusion of losing both of our parents to a disease, seeping heartbreak and lost dreams through a family that once was full of hope.

Despite the crisscrossed emotions, my father stands out as a teacher to me, and he planted a moral code in me that, fortunately, has remained indestructible. Although I have tried at different times to will life another way, the light my Daddy cast has never been totally extinguished.

By the time of his death at the age of 70, my father had taught me not only the necessity of living a life based on honesty, but a life in which faith was the cohesion—and the liberation—from the pain of unexpected turns. No matter what hardships might come to my own life—the heartbreak of first love, the wrenching of divorce, or the terror of almost dying—he would always say, "You must have faith. It is the way it is supposed to be. You can't understand it right now, but someday you will be able to look back and see how it was for the best."

As I grow older, I understand better the quiet arduousness of the life he lived. Though my father sometimes wavered from his moral plumb line, he tried to be true to the principle he knew was right for him (and which he therefore assumed would work for anybody else): that decency was its own reward.

A few years after law school, my father became the youngest appointed judge in our county's history, and my Mama, whose own father had been a Congressman, likes to remember that the politics in the South in the thirties and forties were such that my father was being groomed for a gubernatorial run. It is a known fact that everyone looked up to my father. Almost everybody called him "Judge" and tipped his hat to him when he walked by, and most of the other lawyers in town went to him when they needed some clarification of a hair-splitting law.

A few years after I was born in 1941, my Mama, who looked exactly like Hedy Lamarr, and my Daddy, whose friendliness and reputation more than compensated for his height and skinny frame, suddenly had to move out of our beautiful brick house in the greenest part of town. The sparkling views of my Mama dressed in a long black velvet gown and my Daddy in a black suit and crisp white shirt abruptly ended. The dances they attended at the Country Club with orchestras like Kay Kaiser's continued, but I no longer saw these beautiful gods sweep through our front door to attend them. As a child, I only knew that, suddenly, something was very different. My brother, my parents and I now shared one bedroom in my grandparents' big house at the far end of town.

Despite the tumult and forgotten dreams that my father's disease was reaping, at five years old I did not know what was happening to our family. Now, when I look back on those days at my grandparents' house, I find some of my fondest memories. They remind me again of Scout and her older brother Jem, who would explore the tiny world of their neighborhood every day. My brother, Dwight, and I did the same thing, and on Sunday nights, Daddy would lead the whole family on an adventure.

Sunday nights were the best. After Daddy and I played cards and listened to Sam Spade on the radio, he would stand up tall and laugh, "I know what! Let's all get in the car right now. There's somewhere I want to take you!"

These were the glorious nights. My brother and I would nestle against the scratchy brown upholstery of our four-door Dodge sedan as Daddy drove way across town to what, in 1946, was called "colored town." As soon as he turned off Center Street, he would shut off the car lights, cut the engine, then slide the car next to the curb not far from a small brick church. He'd drape his long arm across the back of the front seat, turn to us children and whisper, "Now, you must be very, very quiet. Don't say a word. Just be very, very quiet and listen."

Within a few minutes, as we huddled in the back of this dark, muffled car parked on a pitch-black street, the music would begin. I would sit up in my seat and lean behind Daddy's shoulders as the throaty, sonorous voices began to rock. We could hear hands clapping and the belly moans of bodies swaying to hymns that were never sung at the church over on Main Street. Sunday night after Sunday night, my Daddy would drive us down there. "Just listen," he would admonish. "Just listen."

Three years after we had moved in with my grandparents, my parents separated, and Daddy took a room in the hotel on Main Street. Sometimes when I visited him there, I'd find him slumped in a chair in his room. Other times he would be dressed up and happy, and he'd ask me to come downstairs and have dinner with him.

It was on one such evening, when I was about 11, that he taught me the kind of bone-chilling lesson that he, more than anyone else, could deliver as a punch to my consciousness. The waitress that night was particularly snappy. She snarled at just about anything Daddy or I said, and she seemed to slam every dish from one place to another. "She's so mean, Daddy," I finally said, "I don't think she's very nice."

My Daddy's eyes flashed as he continued looking at his plate, and without lifting his head, he didn't skip a beat. "Don't you ever let me hear you talk about someone like that again," he said. "You don't know what happened to that woman today. You don't know if her children are sick, if she and her husband might have had an argument this morning before she came to work. You don't know what the truth is, and you have no business ever criticizing someone else."

I was stunned by his words which I knew in the pit of me were correct. In fact, it was this same easy and precise ability of my father's to discern ethical principles that continued to enrich our relationship and fuel our conversations until his death in 1976. For the last 20 years of his life, as he maintained victory in his battle with outside dependencies, his injunctions about appropriate behavior became even more steady and precise. They were also more frequent, and most of them centered on the spiritual deepening that was happening in him and eluding me.

The faith he relied on in times of pain or fear was particularly unfathomable to me as I grew older. "But *how* do you have faith, Daddy?" I would ask well into my 30s and with two children of my own.

"You just have it," he answered evenly.

"But how?" I would sometimes cry with frustration.

"You just have it, honey," he would repeat.

A few years before my father's death, I was devastated by the separation of my marriage and the fact that I had a son and a daughter to bring up, hopefully in less scarring and confusing circumstances than my brother and I had suffered. The strain of being a single parent became too much to bear, and I became more and more depressed. I also suffered massive embolisms for which I was hospitalized for over six weeks. I almost died from the blood clots, and emotionally, I felt worthless and incapable of continuing as a single working parent.

During this difficult time, my father wrote me a letter: "Your illness has made me think many times of a story I once read about some African natives. They had been employed to carry supplies on their backs through a jungle. They would faithfully carry their burdens without any hesitation. Then without any warning, they would sit down and refuse to move. Their employers demanded a reason for their actions. They told their employers that they had to stop and rest until their spirits caught up with them. What a way to say that the burdens had forced them to stop and wait for the restorative power of nature.

"I would not try to hazard a guess as to how long it will take you to get fully restored. *But I do know it will happen.*"

"But how do I have this faith, Daddy?" I asked when I returned home from the hospital. "You just have it, honey," he replied again.

And after his death, I slowly began to understand.

The day my father died was a clear November morning. Shafts of sunlight stood like columns between the tall pines and chestnuts outside the waiting room of his hospital, a special area reserved only for families of patients in the most critical condition. I had flown to North Carolina five days earlier when the phone call came saying that Daddy, age 70 and survivor of two heart attacks, had had a massive stroke. "He's brain dead," the doctor said when I arrived. "Ninety-seven percent of his brain is gone, and so we have him on life-support systems. It's just a matter of time, we don't know how much, but we can only let family members see him, one at a time, for no more than ten minutes."

"How often?" I asked.

"Three times a day," he told me.

So this is it, I thought as my mind whirled under the sudden compression of time. On my first visit with Daddy that night, I had expected to see the tubes hooking him up to machines, but I choked when I saw the white gauze bandages covering his laughing blue eyes. I squeezed his hand and began to talk.

"It's me, Daddy. I made it. I came to see how you're doing." I just kept mumbling hello and holding and kissing his hand and rubbing the white hair back from his tall forehead. "I'm here, Daddy," I kept mumbling, and the tears wouldn't stop.

I kept staring at those gauze bandages wondering what was in his mind when suddenly I felt him squeeze my hand. I looked up to his face and tears were rolling down his cheeks. "Oh, Daddy," I sobbed, "I'm so so sorry this is happening to you. Are you O.K.? Are you O.K.?" And I felt him squeeze my hand once again as the nurse poked her head through the door and said, "It's time."

I couldn't understand how someone brain dead could squeeze my hand or have tears roll down his cheeks. That night I called my cousin, who is a physician, to try to understand. When I asked him if we had to leave the bandages on his eyes, he said yes, that the gauze helps prevent the eyes from drying out.

"But he cried, Glen," I said.

"Are you sure?" my cousin asked.

I was sure, and I was also sure that at some level my Daddy had a glimmer of what was happening to him.

He lived for four more days. He was unable to squeeze my hand after the second day and on the third day, the doctors said that my brother, stepmother, and I would have to decide whether we wanted to leave him on the machines. This was the year of the Karen Quinlan case in which this woman's family was fighting for the right to disconnect her life support and allow her to die, as they saw it, with dignity. We didn't hesitate in our agreement, however, to leave him plugged in. We simply could not impose the alternative decision on someone else's life.

During my visits with Daddy, I would talk, hoping for any tiny physical acknowledgment from him that I was telling him something he needed to hear. Each day he became weaker as his body hollowed under the sheet and his hands grew more limp. I was desperate to understand why he was hanging on.

"What is it, Daddy?" I would ask. "Are you worried about Mama? You know she still loves you. I promise we'll take care of her. Are you worried about me? I'll be O.K., you know that. What is it, Daddy? What is it you want to hear?"

Finally, on my last visit with him, I knew I had searched every plausible situation that I thought might still be troubling him and for which he might be waiting to hear reassurances.

It was early evening and I had run out of things to say or

questions to ask him. It was very, very quiet on the floor that night, and I just stood by the low gate at his side and looked at him. I had run out of tears, and I had run out of words. Out of nowhere, a feeling seemed to tell me to get on my knees. I was shocked—I hadn't done that since I was a child. My studies in theology had convinced me long ago that kneeling was a ritual only for the ignorant or the misinformed.

I also knew that since my father had become sober twenty years earlier, every morning and every evening he had gotten on his knees beside his bed to say thank you. Why this thought came that I should kneel, I don't know, but down I went. I held my father's left hand, bowed my head, and began to sob, "Daddy, I love you. Please forgive me for anything I may have done to knowingly or unknowingly hurt you or anyone else. Daddy, I love you. I am truly sorry, I will always try to be your best daughter. I want you to be happy, too."

As impulsively as I had knelt down, I stood up again and remained by his side, looking up and down his long body covered by the sheet, remembering his beautiful blue eyes under the bandages. I suddenly became aware that he truly was leaving now, and I wanted to know my father, every bit of him, before he left.

I had never seen my father naked, not even bare-chested. He was a very formal, even shy, man, and I occasionally saw him, at most, in a short-sleeved shirt without a tie. Now, I reached down and put both hands under the edge of the sheet lying loosely across his body. Very slowly, I lifted it to see my Daddy. I started at his long, elegant feet, and my eyes moved up his legs, across his hips, up over his stomach, across his rib cage, right up to his shoulders and finally to his handsome face. He was lovely. *This was the man who helped make me,* I thought. Returning my gaze to his thick rib cage, I began to laugh. "So that's where I got this rib cage of mine," I chuckled to myself. "No wonder mine is so big and boxy. Look at his."

Smiling still, I lowered the sheet and walked out of the room feeling peaceful, somehow, for the first time in four days. The next morning as I waited my turn to visit my father again, I was distracted by a little girl in a blue dress who was playing with her grandmother, until I saw my father's physician coming our way. When the doctor reached us, the little girl became still and my heart seemed to stop. He said very quietly, "Your father just died, I'm so sorry."

The only regret I have about the life my father had to live and what he could and couldn't give me is that his disease robbed us of more time together. Rare were the moments in my childhood that he laughed with me or moments in my teenage years when he could counsel me about the pain of jealous friends or the tender side of first dates. Perhaps there are only handfuls of times as a child and young girl when we laughed together or he spent time showing me the world and the kindest ways to live in it. His disease robbed us both. And his lessons, consequently, stand out like the steepest ridges on a mountain.

The first months after his death were the hardest. I was trying to raise two small children. I had few close friends and a remnant of a spiritual life. I was desperately lonely. I felt isolated and inadequate. My mother, who was extremely depressed after a radical mastectomy, could offer little support. I didn't know where to turn.

The compass of my father's guidance was gone, and my own depression told me that either I was incapable of solving my problems or that I was intelligent enough to figure them out all by myself. I was caught in a conundrum that fluctuated between terror on one side and arrogance on the other.

Then one day I remembered little Scout as she waited anxiously for her father, Atticus, to come home from work. She needed to talk to him about a problem that was bothering her. When Atticus finally did come home, they sat down on an old swing on the front porch, and he held her next to his side while she told him what was troubling her.

An idea flashed across my mind: *When you don't know what to do, pretend to call your father and imagine what he would say.* I did it. I imagined dialing his number just as I had done hundreds of other times. I imagined telling my father, sentence by sentence, what was troubling me, and I heard his voice, sentence by sentence, answering me. It worked.

But as I turned inward to deal with my problems, I felt more and more alone and the more I withdrew, the more I relied on just myself—and my father—for help. I didn't consult family or friends, and I had no spiritual life to guide me. I knew something was terribly wrong with me. I began to see that no matter how secure my profession looked or how many relationships I might pretend were serious and fulfilling, I still felt inadequate and lost. I would try different churches, then find an intelligent reason for discounting teachings that asked you to believe without knowing what you would get in return.

For ten years after my father's death, I could find nothing, not even imagined phone conversations, to opiate the vacuum in me that was growing larger as my life grew smaller and smaller. My father was no longer available to counsel, guide, correct, and encourage me. The moral plumb line he passed on to me frayed to its own dark edges, and my self-respect shrank to a pinpoint of light less and less recognizable. At that time my children were in college, and I was physically alone for the first time in my life. I felt totally useless, and everything I tried—travel, glamorous surroundings, professions, and relationships—left me wanting. I felt like a fraud, and I had run out of new things that I thought could make me feel better. I felt too scared to die, and too tired to live.

One morning, feeling completely at a loss, I suddenly heard my Daddy's voice from behind my left shoulder. "I am powerless," his voice said. "I have to ask for help."

There it was. And there he was. One more time. My hands flew across my heart, the wind left my lungs, and I sat absolutely still in a chair. I knew without question and as quietly and as peacefully as the unfolding of a morning that I couldn't keep living my life the way I had. I had to change my actions, and the correct thinking would follow. What I had been doing had not worked. Self-will, as it had proved itself with my father's disease, was now running the risk of obliterating my own life. In that moment, I experienced faith for the first time. I simply knew, deep within, that if I changed my behavior, my life would change for the better. Just as my father had always said, faith was so simple. You simply had it.

After that moment, I quit drinking, I quit smoking, I asked friends for help, and I added daily spiritual practice to my life. I began my own road to recovery, and at various points along the way, I continue to be struck by the quiet power of this man who lived a very simple life in his last twenty years. Each day that I lived with these new actions, my self-respect was restored. The faith that had taken root in my father's lessons now became a flowering reality in my life. Each time I did something that made me feel good about myself, the faith found deeper soil in which to grow.

Today, I am studying Buddhism, and I think my father would understand that, too. As a matter of fact, he would like that the Buddhists give full credit to any path of spiritual conduct that suggests a higher rather than lower code of behavior and leaves no one out.

Recently, I heard the Dalai Lama talking about the "avoidance of the ten non-ethical actions—one of them was the act of lying, one of them was divisive speech. I smiled just like I did when I was a small girl hearing my father say, "You must never, ever lie. No matter what is going on or what caused a thing or what your friends might think, you must never lie. Do you understand?"

Today, it feels like I've come home. When I meditate each morning or I have disagreements with the man I love, I can almost hear my father saying, "You must never, ever criticize another person. You don't know what is going on with him and what is causing him to act this way."

Even more frequently, it seems, I remember those long ago days in our small Southern town. I can still hear my father telling me, at age seven, that no, he didn't think I was smart because of what I had done that day at my lemonade stand. He told me that when Miss Jessie, a black lady we knew, gave me all the money she had, four pennies, I should have given her a whole pack of gum instead of only four sticks. "I am glad you have learned to count," he said, "but I am not proud that you were selfish."

Now, when I think about my father, there is a scene from *To Kill a Mockingbird* that often crosses my mind. Near the end of the film, Atticus is crushed when he loses his case defending a black man who is falsely accused of rape. The entire black community has come to court to see him try to right a wrong, and they occupy the balcony of the courtroom along with six-year-old Scout and her brother, who are sitting next to the town's black minister.

Scout, hanging over the balcony rail to watch her father walk out of the courtroom, does not realize that all of the people around her have risen from their seats as her father begins to leave.

"Scout, stand up," the minister urges.

"Why?" Scout asks.

"Because your father is passing."

It happened, fortunately, the same way for me.

MY FATHER'S ENDURING GIFT—LIFE TRIUMPHS

ANTOINETTE BOSCO

THE LAST MEMORY I have of my father is his feebly waving to me from his hospital bed with a broad smile before fading into yet another of his intermittent states of oblivion, shortly before his death on December 5, 1985.

The day we buried him was cloudy and gray. But as I and my seven brothers and sisters placed our flowers on his coffin at the cemetery, we were suddenly surrounded with light. The sun came out strong, with the full glory of new life. We knew then that dad was smiling at us yet. He wasn't really gone. He was with us and would be always.

Oh that smile of my father's! That smile and his faith in life were the blessings I felt at a young age. One of the first articles I ever wrote, published in a Catholic magazine in 1953, was about my father. I called it "Faith and a Smile." His faith in life—and his smile—sustained him for his 83 years on earth.

Joseph Oppedisano, my father, was no ordinary man. He was a man of considerable courage. When I was a child he would occasionally mention his youth in the southern part of Italy, but then he would become quiet and somber. I always sensed he had undergone a trauma at some point in his early life. It wasn't until I was in my late 30's that he poured out his story; we sat up talking into the early morning hours.

He was only 13 years old when he suddenly had to leave his home near Reggio, Calabria. Someone in the village had accused him of a very serious crime, the assault of a well-known, wealthy man. In 1915, no laws existed in southern Italy to protect the poorer people like my father. A person could be set up, thrown into prison, and left to rot, merely at the accusation of someone who had clout with the local police. Rather than have their youngest son risk that fate, my grandparents sent him off into the world to stay free and make a new life for himself.

I try to imagine this child of 13, heading north through Italy and France as World War I was raging, trying to survive against a language barrier, with no money and no skills. I feel tremendous admiration for the strength he found to help him reach his goal of getting to America. It took him three years to earn enough money for the boat passage, but at age 16, he made it. He always talked about how, when he arrived at Ellis Island, he thanked God for helping him get to the "land of gold."

It was the beginning of his new life. He worked hard, learned the butcher trade, married a beautiful young woman named Mary, started his business, and raised a family of eight children. He never spoke of America without calling it "the best country in the world."

My father told me that when he was starving in France, he once stole a loaf of bread. "That's why," he said, "if anyone comes into my store hungry, I can't refuse them." I witnessed that kindness and generosity many times over the years as countless people walked out of his store with a bag of food paid for only with a thank you.

My personal thank-you to my father is a deep and lasting one. He gave me the spirit and attitude that life is great and you should never give up on it. He recognized that people live on two levels—the acquisitive and the inquisitive—and he placed highest value on the latter.

From the time I was a little girl, he would tell me, "Antoinette, they can take anything away from you, but an education, they can't take away." In spite of the fact that he was an Italian man, bound by a tradition which saw a woman's place in the home, not the classroom, he dared to be different when it came to education. He always spoke intensely about the need for me to go to school and he expected from me school performance that was not just good, but brilliant.

If I came home from school with a 98 average, he would ask, "Why wasn't it 100?" And when, in defense, I would counter that this was the highest report card in the class, he countered even faster, "So you have a class of dumbbells." What he clearly communicated was his confidence in me, his belief that I was brighter than most of my classmates and that I should become *somebody* when I became an adult. He gave me a sense of self-esteem very early in my life.

My father supported not only my desire to go to college, but also my decision to enter a man's field, pre-med studies, which was rare for a woman in the late 1940's. And when it turned out that we simply didn't have the clout or money for medical school, he hurt as much as I did.

In communicating to me his belief that I had an intellect and capabilities that could stretch far, my father gave me the tools I needed for later life—to choose independence, accept responsibility for supporting myself and my children as a single mother, to believe in my own ability to achieve, and never to be smug about accomplishments.

I remember many occasions in my pre-teen years when my father related to me in a special way. But two really stand out.

The first was in the summer of 1937, Depression time, when hard-working people were doing all they could just to keep body and soul together. I was nine and left home for the first time to spend a month with my Aunt Justina and Uncle Jimmy.

There wasn't much to do in the little town of Sidney in upstate New York, where Uncle Jimmy had a job as a crossing guard at the railroad tracks. I read a lot of books and brought lunch to Uncle Jimmy every day at noon. Sometimes I stayed with him while we waited for the train to hoot, signaling him to swing his red lamp and warn traffic to stop. There was a movie in town that I really wanted to see, but I couldn't go because it cost 10 cents and I had no money.

I was only there about two weeks, feeling terribly lonely for my parents, my sister Rosemary and my one-year-old brother Joe, when the letter came. It was from my father. He wrote that he was keeping busy working, that Joey was walking and doing cute things. He said he missed me and he wanted me to have some fun, to go shopping and buy something for myself. In the envelope was a dollar. A dollar! I had never seen so much money in my hand. And during the Depression, that was a lot of money for a 9-year-old girl to have.

I spent the dollar carefully. I lit two candles in church, at 5 cents each, bought ice cream cones for my aunt, my uncle and myself, bought a powder puff for my aunt, and a writing pad, envelope and stamp so I could thank my father. Then, with great excitement, I went to the movies by myself, paying the matinee price of 10 cents, and enjoying the antics of Joe E. Brown and Martha Raye.

The incident, of course, wasn't about shopping, ice cream and movies. It was about how truly I felt my father's love for me, how internalized that gift of himself became.

The second incident in which my father and I shared a special relationship was much different. It happened at Christmas time. I was 12 that December and just beginning to move out of the innocence of childhood and into a new awareness that the adult world held some painful mysteries I would rather not yet know about.

My brother Jimmy had been born on September 30 of that year, and he had almost died four weeks later. I still remember my mother's screams when she went to nurse him and found him barely breathing. We had no phone back then, so my sister Rosemary ran to a neighbor's house and phoned a doctor and my father. I ran two blocks to the rectory and got Father Hogan to come with me. Jimmy had not yet been baptized, and for Catholics, the situation was most serious. Back then we feared that if a baby died without baptism, he or she would never go to Heaven, only to a place called Limbo.

I can still see tiny Jimmy on a pillow on the dining-room table, with Father Hogan quickly giving him conditional baptism while the doctor gave him artificial respiration. When the doctor put my mother and Jimmy into his car and drove to the hospital—his left hand steering and his right hand continuing the artificial respiration—I started to shake. My father got home and I could see his breaking heart by the expression on his face as he got back into the car to go to the hospital. I cried with a pain I had never experienced before, facing the possibility that I might lose the little brother I so dearly loved.

By Christmas Day I had changed. I started to notice subtle things, like my mother's moods and my father's excessive smoking. The day was not pleasant. We had a houseful of cousins, and mother could not hide her resentment that she was stuck with the gigantic chore of cooking. Jimmy was still frail and we kept him isolated from the crowd. I hovered over him like the proverbial mother hen.

At about four in the afternoon my father, who had not seemed himself all day, told me to go to the deli across the street and get him some cigarettes. The store was empty except for the owner's daughter. As I came in the phone rang. It was her boyfriend, and since I was just a 12-year-old kid, she had no qualms about keeping me waiting before she handed me the cigarettes.

When I got back to the house, my father was waiting for me at the door. Almost shaking with rage because of my delay, which he assumed was my fault, he slapped me, moving me through three rooms with his blows until I landed against a kitchen wall.

I was literally in a state of shock. I did not cry. I glared at him in disbelief and confusion and anger. It was the first time—and last— that he ever hit me. I didn't know what had happened to him to make him react that way.

An hour later, his remorse evident, my father tried to be nice to me, offering to take me to a movie. Haughtily, I said no. He had spoiled my holiday and I needed time to forgive him.

A few days later my mother told me that my father had gotten a telegram on Christmas informing him that his mother—my grand-mother who lived in Italy and whom I had never met—had died. That's why he had been so upset, she said.

Then I cried for my father, because I understood, at least in part, his suffering. I had only a few weeks earlier faced the possibility of my baby brother's death and felt the agony. What pain he must have experienced knowing he had not seen his mother since he was 13 and now could never see her again.

For the first time in my young life, I learned the meaning of compassion. Later, when my father could talk about his terrible loss, he helped me understand how we either can fall apart from the blows of life, or we can use them to help us become more human. He wanted me to choose the latter. We hugged each other, merging our separate traumas so they became one. My forgiveness and the revelation from this experience were both huge and permanent.

No story about my father would be complete without remembering his love of music. I was only seven when he came home from
work one day and with evident excitement told me and my sister
Rosemary, who was nine, that he had a wonderful surprise for us. He
was getting us a piano! This was the Depression era and somehow my
father, who made $35 a week as a butcher for the Albany Public
Market, had managed to save $25, the cost of the secondhand,
upright piano.

Three days before it was to be delivered, my father waited on a
customer, an old woman, whose purchase came to $1. Somewhat
embarrassed, she asked my father if he could cut her meat by a few
ounces to make it just 90 cents' worth. All she had was $1 and she
needed 10 cents for the bus to get home.

My father, empathizing with her, gave her the $1 package,
charging her 90 cents. She thanked him and when she turned away,
he took 10 cents out of his own pocket to make up the difference.

All the while, his boss had been watching. When the woman
was out of hearing range, he bellowed at my father that this was no
way to run a store. Business was business. Charity was something
else and not allowed in his store. My father, a proud and kind man
who could not believe what he was hearing, responded that he
couldn't work for a man who had no heart. He quit his job
then and there.

My father came home from work early that day and, obviously
dejected, told us that the piano wasn't coming. We needed the $25 he
had saved to live on until he found another job. We were sorry about
the piano, but so proud of our father, who by his action, taught us
the meaning of caring for another human being, even a stranger. A
few years later, my father came home with a musical instrument he
could afford—an accordion. Rosemary and I, and eventually my
brother Joe, learned to play well. When we could afford it, he bought

a piano, too. We always had music in the house, and, with daddy's encouragement, we grew up going to concerts and operas.

Six months before my father turned 83, I had to face the fact that he had made the irreversible shift to old age. I knew it had happened when he asked me, "Antoinette, where's your husband? I haven't seen him lately." I reminded him gently that he hadn't seen him in 19 years because that was how long we had been divorced. I was glad Daddy didn't notice the tears in my eyes.

I never wanted to face the day when one of my parents would get old. We always laughed at age, as if it didn't exist. We said it was a number, something we hang on a calendar, not on ourselves. My parents were always youthful, looking more at times like my brother and sister than my mother and father.

Both had incredible energy and a philosophy that you should never walk when you can run. My father reached 80 still "feeling like 20," a phrase I'd heard him use all his life.

But that 80th birthday was the turning point for him, the age when he began to slow down. Instead of going out for walks, he started to lift himself from one chair only to walk to another. He began to fall down frequently.

Now and then his face would grow tight, as if in response to pain. He would admit, if you pressed him, that his back or his leg hurt "a little," but it was never enough to see a doctor. He started to grow quieter, not communicating very much, though he ate, slept, and watched television. He smiled and cried when I visited him, but little by little, I realized he wasn't with us, not really. His mind was in the past, periodically going further and further back. It was as if he were preparing himself for the final reversal—getting ready to leave this world.

When he was younger, my father often would be unpredictable, getting angry and then the next minute growing loving and thoughtful. Now I look back and wonder if the wild side of him was his defense. Maybe he learned to show occasional belligerence as a mark of strength in order to make it as a 16-year-old immigrant to the United States.

But it seemed that now, since it was no longer necessary for him to "make it," his defenses could come down, exposing his true nature—the soft and emotional man in front of me. And oh, how much I learned about him, mainly his incredible capacity to bear his own pain, and his refusal to be a burden. I never once heard him complain of his hurts and discomforts. His strength turned inward. The man who had been authoritative, forceful, always in charge, became this gentle person, asking nothing, making no demands, quietly but strongly moving into his final journey. People always said I "took after" my father, and to this day I pray that I advance in age in the way that he did.

When my father died, I remembered his generosity—but it was my brother Joe who remembered the *spindle*. He told the story to the hundreds of relatives and friends who came to my father's funeral.

Today, businesses have sophisticated ways of keeping track of who owes how much money. "But in those days, in our store, we had the spindle, where each night we fastened together strips of wrapping paper on which were recorded the cash register reading and the change count in the coin drawers."

And then my brother reminded us of "the other scraps of wrapping paper on the spindle, each one containing a customer's name and varying dollar amounts. You see," he continued, "these slips represented people in the hurtful and uncomfortable position of having too much month left at the end of their money.

"And sometimes the spindle would be thick with these 'credit' notes. But more often than nor, many of those slips with the names of people and the amounts owed would somehow become lost, or would turn up as crumpled papers to be thrown out with the old sawdust and the trash."

Joe shared his conclusion with us: "God uses his own measuring stick to evaluate his creatures. And I understand that if you observe very carefully, you will see that this [measuring stick] looks suspiciously like a gigantic, cosmic spindle to which are fastened all of those curiously lost and crumpled papers of our dad's life, each one convertible into some celestial building materials.

"And so," said my brother, "one day, when we join our dad, we shouldn't be surprised to find that he has the largest and most magnificent mansion among the 'many mansions' Jesus said are in his 'Father's house.'"

None of us have ever forgotten that spindle!

While I was not surprised that my brother would talk of my father's many kindnesses at his funeral Mass, he took me by surprise when he said, "And now, let's talk about the gift of music. . . ." He pointed out all of us, children and grandchildren, who are musicians—his own son Joe, a fine keyboardist, my sister Jeannette, a blues singer, my daughter Maria, an opera singer, Rosemary's son John, a professional bassist, my son Frank, a guitarist, and himself, for a quarter century, the leader of a combo.

And then he asked, "But who sang the first song?"

As tears welled up in me, so did my gratitude to my father. My brother's question had peeled away fifty years, bringing me back to the Depression days. I felt again the mourning for the loss of the $25 piano we never got because of my father's choice to live by his values. But now I could feel something deeper—a tremendous love for that young immigrant, a man of 33, so drawn to music that the only money he had been able to save was to be spent on a piano, to pass on his love for the harmonies of song to his young daughters.

Yet, he had placed greater importance on the pervasive harmony that should be shared by all human beings—namely caring—even if it is a stranger who needs only a dime.

When my brother asked, "Who sang the first song?" I could have shouted, "Our father did!" For not only did he give us the gift of music, he sang a 10-cent song that will resound in our hearts forever.

For all he gave us, Dad lives in us, more alive than ever as the years pass on. *Bravissimo, Papa.*

FROM SOPHIA:
LIVING AND LOVING
SOPHIA LOREN WITH
A.E. HOTCHNER

I WAS ON A sound stage in Rome making *A Special Day* when my sister unexpectedly came to tell me that our father was in serious condition in the hospital. I immediately left with her. My father was in a room with three other patients. He looked gaunt and wasted, and at first I feared that we had come too late.

"We are here, Papa," Maria said, "Sophia and me."

On hearing our voices, he opened his eyes and managed a slight smile. "*Sono felice,*" he said, which means, I am happy. He closed his eyes. He was heavily drugged for his pain, and after a short while I left. I would have stayed longer, but the other patients in the room had visitors who had recognized me and I felt awkward. I just wanted to be an ordinary person visiting her sick father, not a movie star being set upon by everyone in the room and a few nurses and interns to boot. It was certainly not the time and place for it. But before I left, I managed to have a talk with the woman whom my father had lived with for the past ten years, a very nice German woman named Carol, who had been quietly sitting in the corner. She was taking my father's condition very hard. She had been completely devoted to him and he was the only life she had.

That evening, my thoughts would not leave my father. In a way, strange to say, he was the most important man in my life. I had spent my life seeking surrogates for him—in Carlo, the husband who fathers me, in de Sica, who fathered me as a director, and so forth. Despite all the grandiose gifts I had received in my life, that little blue auto my father gave me with my name on it retained a special place in my memory.

My sister, who has a much more forgiving heart than I, had seen him often, and it was she who told me about his illness and about how, when he felt well enough to leave his flat, he would go to movie houses that were showing my films and sit for endless hours watching me. I wondered what went through his mind as he sat alone in the dark observing me on the screen. Whether he ever recalled the early days of our existence when he had not only turned his back on us but in a curious way tried to punish us. That he refused to give Maria his name in that Pozzuoli courtroom; that he made me pay my first million lire for it, and then, a year later, tried to repudiate the agreement—in order to get another payment out of me, I presume. That he even made it difficult for me to collect the three thousand lire a month ($4.60) which, for a few months of my life, he was obligated to pay for my support. And did he recall condemning us to the police in an attempt to run us out of Rome, back to Pozzuoli? Did he have any memory of, or guilt about, all the times my mother asked for his help when we were starving?

I did not expect him to understand the pain of a young girl branded as illegitimate, nor even the raw shame of his wife screaming at me in front of all those *Quo Vadis* people, "You're not a Scicolone!

I am! I'm the only Scicolone here!" But surely he must have recalled with some contrition the libel suit. Surely some guilt that he sued his own daughter for libeling his reputation when he himself had branded her reputation with the stigma of illegitimacy. That lawsuit had roused anger in me, and for a time I hated my father for what he had done. But as I got older and learned more about people, I came to realize that hate is an acid that eats away—not the person hated but the one who hates.

I had also faced reality about my father: he was what he was, and festering criminations about him was pointless. As my viewpoint about him changed, so did my emotions. I no longer had any hate or scorn for him—only pity. I felt sad for him because . . . he could have had a rewarding and fruitful life, and instead he spurned it, spurned the people who wanted to love him, who cared about him, and he seemed always to be living against himself. A self-defeatist. Destructive. Needlessly creating problems that nurtured his bitterness and hostility. I thank God I inherited none of that from him. I don't want to destroy myself or anyone else. My nature is to give and be involved, without a thought to receiving anything for myself. This wellspring of generous giving probably contributes much to my acting, for what is true acting except the ability of the actor to give his emotions and feelings to his audience?

So I pitied my father who couldn't give affection and love to his women and the children whom he brought into his life. Perhaps toward the end he had a glimmer of this. Not long before he went to the hospital, at his request my sister arranged for me to visit him in his apartment in Rome. I had not seen him for many years, and I had never been to a place he lived in. I found him much older than his years. I believe he was suffering from cancer. He was very pleased to see me and took me all around the flat showing me his possessions and mementos.

We did not have much to talk about, but it mattered a great deal to him that I see everything in his home. When it was time to leave, and we stood in the doorway saying good-bye, he took one of my hands in his and said, "Lella, I am very proud of you."

That was the only affectionate thing he ever said to me.

*****

A short time after my first visit to the hospital, Maria again came to fetch me. "Come quickly," she said, "Papa is dying. Quickly!"

My father had been moved to a private room. Several of his relatives stood in a cluster at the far side of the room. And to my amazement, my mother was present. She has a terrible fear of death. She never goes to hospitals or funerals. She had not seen my father for years, but the fatal fascination he had for her had held true even to his death. She had borne him two daughters and he had been the only man she had ever lived with. However she may condemn him, he was the one and only love of her life. And now she had defied her obsessive death-fear to be present at his demise.

Also present was the Carol woman. But my father's first wife, Nella Rivolta, the mother of his two sons, was not there. Nor did she come to his funeral.

My father had an oxygen mask on his face, and an attendant stood beside the bed, monitoring the breathing apparatus. Seated on one side of the bed was a handsome young man, thirty years or so of age, who was holding one of my father's hands in both of his. The young man looked familiar, like someone I had known well a long time ago. Carol led me to the bed and introduced us. Giuseppe was his name, the younger of my father's two sons. He shyly acknowledged the introduction. I felt strange, meeting my brother for the first time at my father's deathbed.

I sat down on the opposite side of the bed and took my father's other hand. I looked across at Giuseppe, joined as we were by my father's hands. There was a soft, gentle quality to his face. I had an illusion that we were old friends. There was a shyness about him with which I identified.

I turned my attention to my father's anguished breathing. Giuseppe had shifted around to look at the monitor beside the bed. It was going erratically. My father's hand felt cold and inert in mine. Life was running out of him.

My mother never took her eyes off my father. Carol sat in the corner, her face covered with her hands. My sister stood beside my mother, watching the breathing machine.

And then the attendant turned off the oxygen and my father was dead. I had never seen anyone die before. The attendant took the mask off my father's face, and placing both his hands on my father's chest, he gave a mighty shove, pushing the last of the oxygen from my father's body.

Carol started to weep. Giuseppe released my father's hand and walked over to the window. I looked at my father's face, now free of the oxygen mask, and I felt compelled to touch his cheek with my fingertips.

"*Ciao, Papa,*" I said, and welcome into my heart forever.

My mother had started to cry, not covering her face, letting the tears run freely. My sister, too, was weeping, but she had turned her back to the bed and was weeping against the wall.

I went over to the window where Giuseppe was standing, looking up at the sky. He was striving to hold back his tears. And so was I. Unlike me, as a child Giuseppe had lived with my father, so I guess he felt his loss more keenly. He turned and looked at me; it was a look of distress, of need. I reached out to him and he collapsed against me releasing his tears. As did I. I put my arms around him and comforted him and felt very much his sister.

United in our sorrow, embraced, shedding common tears, I felt a surge of love for this new brother of mine who wept in my arms. How ironic that at his death, my father, who had given me so little in life, had left me a priceless legacy—a brother. I felt an eerie exultation, as if this young man had risen from the corpse of my father, his flesh and blood, to bring to me the kind of kinship that I had never had with my father.

So there in his death room, I both grieved for my father's demise and experienced the throb of encountering new life. It was a moment of great meaning for me, which will endure for the rest of my life.

FROM THE BOOKMAKER'S DAUGHTER

SHIRLEY ABBOTT

THE NIGHT MY FATHER died, I stayed at the hospital with him, like the dutiful daughter I had ceased to be. My mother had telephoned me three days earlier. "Daddy's awfully bad. But don't come yet. We've got him in the hospital. He's feeling a little better today. You never can tell with this old diabetes. I think he's had a small stroke." Mother thought I ought not to leave my husband, my job. So I telegraphed a plant, and when she urgently summoned me and I finally arrived, exhausted and then hours late because of canceled flights and other problems, this plant, an azalea pink as spring, sat on the table beside his bed, the only flowers he had. I bent over him, squeezed his hands, patted his pallid cheeks, stroked his head until his eyes opened. He said nothing but gestured weakly toward the azalea and smiled.

Local etiquette, indeed ethics, requires that no family member be left alone in a hospital room for so much as a minute. A blood

relation or spouse must sit round the clock with the sick and the
dying; a uniformed professional at a nurse's station is no substitute.
Since my mother had already sat up for two nights, I persuaded her to
go home and allow me to keep the vigil that night. She agreed, feeling
encouraged by my arrival and his smile, and by his having willingly
swallowed a glass of water and some ice cream that afternoon.
Cautioning me to offer nourishment frequently and not to allow
him to pull out his catheter, which he had done several times already,
she departed.

Scarcely had the door closed behind her when an orderly came
into the room with a suctioning machine. I did not yet believe my
father was dying, although he hadn't spoken for two days and was
having breathing difficulties. "Here we go, Pop," the orderly said,
wielding the brutal mechanism like a vacuum cleaner. I turned to the
young man (younger than I was) in astonishment. Nobody in all my
father's life had ever called him Pop. "This man is Mr. Abbott. You
ought to call him Mr. Abbott." But the orderly did not reply.

I offered my father water through a straw, pleaded with him to
take a little ice cream off his supper tray, but he shut his eyes. I
wondered suddenly if his first wife was still alive, and whether her
letters still caused havoc. Imogene no doubt remembered my father as
I saw him, perversely, even now; six feet tall, slender, his feet planted
defiantly on the front steps of his parents' house, as in the old
photograph I used to study, the one in Grandma's candy box. As I
watched him breathe, I summoned—and quickly cast aside—certain
memories that surged forward. I'd never seen him handsome, blond,
and slender. He was gray-haired by the time I was born, overweight
until misfortune had wasted him. And yet he danced before my eyes
like the prince in a ballet. He certainly had fooled me about his looks.

The month was April, and it rained all night. Because he seemed
so peacefully asleep, I stationed myself in the easy chair, mercifully

provided, where I dozed and woke and the rain still fell, washing down the walls of the hospital, running in rivers, sheets, so that it was impossible to see the streetlights outside. I visited my father's bedside, offering water, murmuring questions about his state of health. I knew the circumstances called for tears, but my serenity was unshakable, my eyes were dry. I tried to make a mental movie of my father taking care of me, but no movie rolled, only the sound of the copious rain, as though the dark sky were equipped with faucets. "What will you miss most about your father?" some voice queried as I dozed. "I'll miss that azalea," I replied, pointing to the plant. "I intend to set out that azalea in my mother's yard," I added illogically. "Next spring it will bloom, so beautiful, azaleas." And finally I fell deeply asleep.

I awoke about dawn—the rain had not let up—to find him looking at me. I went to his bedside. "Daddy." I bent toward his ear. "Do you want anything?" I saw that the sheet was off him. He was quite naked. During the night he had ripped the catheter from his penis, the act of disobedience my mother had begged me to prevent, and now he had done this thing in the night while I slept. The tears came to my eyes at last. How painful it must have been, that cruel tube with the tiny balloon at its upper end! Had he cried out while I slept? (Some terrible association leapt into my mind, crushing me with guilt: oh yes, the disciples snoring while Jesus prepared to die!) Poor limp, dark penis. Out of this had sprung the molecules that made me. Thou shalt not look upon thy father's nakedness. I covered him gently with the sheet. I would give him water through the little plastic straw, and I poured it into a glass. I'd get the nurse to replace the catheter. Then, when I touched his cheek, I saw that he was dead. I went out of the room, shut the door, and leaned against it.

After a time the night nurse discovered me, went briefly inside, and returned to lead me away. "You sit down here, honey. What's Velma's phone number? Let me make that call for you. We need to get her back up here. Which mortuary you want me to call, Gross or Carruthers? We have to do it now, baby, it can't be helped. That's what we have to do. Don't you fret, they'll take good care of him." She telephoned my mother and told her the story: "I'd come on back up here if I was you, Miz Abbott, I think he may be getting a little worse."

Later that day, Mother and I went to the funeral home to make the arrangements. I had read the recent best-selling book by Jessica Mitford about the wiles of undertakers and the foolishness of Americans when it came to death and burial, and I was spoiling for a fight, but when we went to inspect caskets in the showroom, with twenty open boxes like new cars, it was hard to pick the cheapest. Mother was accustomed to picking the cheapest, though, and needed no help from me to resist the sales talk on costly containers that were guaranteed waterproof. She wrote the check and made arrangements to buy two plots, and then we hurried home. By now the phone was ringing, and the women surged into the house, setting things to rights, vacuuming and dusting, changing the bed linen, receiving dishes of food that were delivered to the door, with the name of the donor taped considerately to the bottom so that the dish could be returned.

Soon a huge coffee urn arrived and was set in action; soon every available surface was covered with baked hams, plates of fried chicken, vegetables of every description, cakes, pies, salads. "Stay and eat," the women admonished, as families arrived on condolence calls. And my mother greeted each arrival at the door, weeping briefly on people's shoulders as they hugged and kissed her, exclaiming over the three-bean salads and the heavenly hash, or the sponge cakes, or the pound cans of coffee. Flowers arrived, too, stiff arrangements of chrysanthemums, gladioluses, thrifty kinds of flowers that last for two weeks. Soon the table lamps had to be set on the floor to make room for them. Their bitter fragrance competed with the perking coffee. All was quickly in place: callers occupying every available chair, balancing huge plates of food and coffee cups as they spoke of nothing in particular (for it is not good manners to speak of the dead at such gatherings), the women washing dishes at the sink (for not so much as a coffee cup may be left for the bereaved to deal with)—a gathering of plenty and good will that blotted out death, a ritual that must take place whether the widow and orphans are upright and smiling or unconscious with grief in the next room.

The funeral food, the ritual partaking of each dish, the soft voices talking recipes or the weather or the price of groceries, the square womanly hands in the hot suds at the sink, the arms extended, the gentleness of those who had come to watch over us so that despair was kept at bay outside the door and grief would descend by slow degrees— these offerings had the force and beauty of a sacrament. I could not discount these gestures or tell these kindly, well-meaning souls to go away. But among them I was my father's only friend, an alien as he had been. I thought of a hungry young man leaping from a boxcar near Laramie, Wyoming, of him and Mike reciting poetry in the Chicago streets, of the ragged cabbie who'd had fourteen different jobs already by the time he was twenty-five, of his hands loosening Imogene's red hair, young bodies limb to limb in long and rapturous bliss, as Oscar Wilde so decorously put it, of a bootlegger rounding the curves of a lonely road on two wheels with the cops not far behind him, of a child who called himself by the names of Greek heroes driving a milk cart through the streets of Goshen, Indiana, at dawn. In the bookcase, now wedged into a corner of the tiny living room, the worn copies of the *Iliad* and the *Odyssey*, the matched volumes of Edward Gibbon lined up like English gentlemen in a club, the Oscar Wilde, the Casanova that had taught me the motions of love, the volumes elegantly inscribed from Mike, all these emblems of learning, these foreign voices—these rooms in my father's heart that only I had tried to enter—silently mocked this pious enterprise. I became so vividly aware of my father's outcast state that I could not bite into the fried chicken or the seven-layer coconut cake or even swallow the coffee. I was dizzy, ill. I yearned for a shot of whiskey, the good fiery whiskey that he used to down each morning on his way to work. But no whiskey was offered at this wake. . . .

At some funerals, the mourners are content. It is possible to cite the good deeds, the offices held, the churches tithed to, the children begotten and raised, the grandchildren now making their way in the world, the kindnesses remembered from a life completed. (A good story, with an ending, even if shot with falsehoods.) And there are the other funerals, the kind that make ghosts. This particular horse race was over, and there was no purse. We put him in the cemetery lot that we had paid for the previous day, and laid his pall—a blanket of red carnations my mother had selected—over the raw earth. The mourners, few in number, were Mother's relatives and friends, or the parents of high school friends of mine who had known him through me. Not one bookie or gambler or con artist or crooked politician remembered Hat that day. Perhaps they too were dead.

"In the beginning was the Word, and the Word was God, and the Word was with God." I had asked the preacher to read that at the graveside, and he did; an odd selection, people must have thought, and hardly funereal. Escorting my mother to the undertaker's black limousine, I felt only relief as the service ended and the gravedigger arrived to fill in the hole and finish the job. . . .

Now my father's grave is old, the best kind of grave, to be visited in serenity on a lovely fall or spring afternoon. I never took my daughters to that cemetery as children, but now that they are adults, or nearly, I have taken them once or twice to stand with me at my parents' grave. "Our Daddy." "Beloved wife and mother." I go often to Hot Springs, and whether I arrive in some low-flying two-engine plane from Little Rock, barely clearing the mountaintops, or by highway, rolling up Malvern Avenue past where the old McLaughlin mansion stood, I am propelled by a deep and ineradicable sense of home, though in fact I own nothing here and have nowhere in particular to hang my toothbrush. The sight of the bluish hills curving amply like old women sleeping on their daybeds, as I conceived them to be in my childhood, gladdens and heartens me. I am a stranger here, but this place is mine.

The streets have been altered; indeed, the city I walked as a schoolgirl exists largely in my head. The high school is no longer the high school. The hospital my father died in is no longer a hospital. The bathhouses, except for one, no longer offer baths. One of the elegant old structures has been restored as a museum. The Southern Club is no longer a gambling den but Josephine Tussaud's Wax Museum. On the treads of the staircase that I once climbed wearing my Shirley Temple dress and with my hair in corkscrews stand so-real-they-talk images of Clark Gable, Mae West, and Sophia Loren, among others. In fact they are garish and unreal, in spite of the surrounding hoopla about the "wax-makers' art." At the top of the stairs is a waxen replica of the Last Supper, and above it, in the archway framing the once grand entrance to the gaming room, hangs the slick white body of the crucified Christ: no blood, no sweat, and no genitals under the modest loincloth, of course. Leering companionably from a corner, however, is a life-size Al Capone, chewing a fat cigar. Nearby, the voice of Franklin D. Roosevelt emerges from a 1940s radio, ceaselessly, inexplicably announcing the bombing of Pearl Harbor. Owney Madden has not made it into the waxworks, unfortunately, nor Earl Witt, nor Leo P. McLaughlin. Investigating this place recently, I glanced upward and was overjoyed to see that the ancient domed ceiling with its great chandelier is still in place. Downstairs, in the Southern Grill, where vicious criminals once convivially downed their oysters and lighted their cigars with ten-dollar bills, is the wax museum ticket booth and souvenir shop, which, in the spirit of the good old days, nicks you a pretty penny for a leaflet and a T-shirt.

The auction houses are still in business, with the same gilt statuary and the auctioneers still yodeling in the twilight about their works of art. The Arlington Hotel, carefully restored and maintained but otherwise exactly as I remember it, presides over the city in turreted, verandahed grandeur, its facade turned toward the racetrack, which attracts hundreds of thousands of customers now and even stays open Sundays, Baptists or no Baptists. (So far as I know, Hot Springs makes its living these days out of tourists and the annual race meet. The splendid climate and low cost of living have also made it a popular place to retire.) In the park and along the avenue, our ancient magnolia trees bloom and shed their velvet petals, and the willows waft their foliage like delicate arms in the summer breeze. By its very existence, this place deconstructs and demolishes the American dream of virtue and hard work crowned by success, as well as all platitudes and cant about the democratic process and small-town American life. After an upbringing here, New York City politics, or Watergate, or even the savings and loan scandal, could hardly come as a surprise.

In the tales that constituted his legacy to me, my father's favorite character was himself—Hat, the adventurer caught in misfortune's web, the misfit, the man of intellect, the reader among illiterates, the outsider. He too was an unraveler of myths, even as he furiously knitted them, ensnaring me in the mythologies he based his life on. Yet he also taught me that fathers are not all-powerful—a useful concept for the times I grew to maturity in. He taught me that a flawed patriarch such as himself may actually prefer a daughter to a son. ("I never wanted a boy, I wanted you" has brought me through many a trial.) For some of us, as my father so ardently believed, true salvation can be found only on the printed page—as in the books he read and the books he surely would have written had he been a bookmaker of another kind.

DAD SCATTERED

JANET BURROWAY

THE CORPSE WAS NOBODY I knew. I'm told this is a common feeling. It was skinny, which he never was, and his remaining flesh had thinned and contracted so that although it ought to have been rucked about his jaw it was not; it was taut, like paper wet-shrunk over the balsa bones of a model plane. They had unaccountably repeated that his "color was good"—Gladys who watched him dwindle, the oncologist who pronounced him untreatable, the girl aide who folded his stiff legs in her golden arm to lever him into the wheelchair while the cells ate themselves from the lymph nodes outward, through the roof of his mouth, all down the marrow, while the white corpuscles multiplied amuck to burn his heart with the final indigestion. Even Aunt Jessie, sister as heroine, saying, "Don't wait too long, it won't be long," added, "His color is still good."

All the same, now he was gray. The half-moons of his fingernails were slate, I, yes, turned down the cover to see his hands. He was still warm. I hadn't missed his death my more than half an hour. I lay my cheek against his forehead and felt nothing. I forgot that one feels nothing and I felt: nothing, nothing. I thought coolly: everyone goes through this, sooner or later, more or less. A keening sound came from me—false, effective. I recognized it as an appropriate sound.

You will think I mean that I felt numb, but I did not: numb is a feeling. I felt the paper warmth. The hard proximity of his skull beneath it. I murmured some words which I knew to be false but which would have been the true words I would have murmured had I not been false. Aunt Jessie was there. It later occurred to me that he, Dad, was there.

Now for the moment it has come down to this: a brown carton, smaller than a whiskey carton, on the deep mint plush between Bud and me. "I *hate* that carpet," Gladys said viciously before she went to bed. "It shows every footprint!" Dad has been dead a month but his ashes have not yet been received by the Neptune Society in California. I look for his footprints in the carpet pile even though I vacuumed this morning. I have been in Phoenix since Thursday and have emptied the closet, trashed the ancient toiletries, boxed the clothes for Goodwill, sorted papers into *garbage, important,* and *curiosity.* Jenny will get the woodworking tools; the machine tools will be sold. Tim will have the tartan scarf and Alex, the Dior robe. Gladys will get the stocks, the canoe will go to the Boy Scouts, and I have gathered into this carton what I think Bud and I should look over together. Bud arrived at noon and already the three of us, Gladys and he and I, have settled the formalities of the small inheritance. Since the will was declared void, we agreed on splitting it three equal ways. The lawyer remarked on our amiability. "I've known— literally—families that fought over a toothbrush." Now Gladys, unamiable, has gone to bed, and Bud and I are here assembled to see if a toothbrush will emerge.

"This stop watch," I begin arbitrarily. "I can't figure out where it came from. I never saw it; I don't know if it was his or not."

I begin arbitrarily. I use the term "now" loosely, and variously. I choose this point on the green plush as "now" but might choose any other because tense itself is a fiction. Really, everything is past. At Christmas Gladys will say, "I keep thinking he's in the bedroom, or he's run down to the store. Is that crazy?" Over a course of months I will still be expecting him to die. An airport pager calling for some other Janet, the phone ringing at any slightly out-of-the-ordinary hour, myself surfacing from a dream at dawn—there will be that minute clench in the stomach that represents a readying for the blow. Then immediately I will remember that there's nothing left to fear. The awful is already over. In February I will see, in London, a Morgan roadster, and develop the full intention of asking Dad what he thinks of the Morgan as a car.

However, for the moment, it has come down to this: a box of bric-a-brac, a life's debris, the watch that may or may not have been his and will now become the property of this or that other. What is surprising about his belongings is that there are so few of them. He lived for invention, making, tools, construction. He loved manufacture, advertising, a gimmick, a thingmabob. He doted on rivets, rubber, templates, glue. He was the only man I ever knew excited by the doohickeys of daily maintenance: oil change, furnace filters, rust removers, saddle soap. If that is who he was, why did he not invest in more Turtle Wax, more toggle bolts and caulk guns we could claim for our inheritance?

In fact there are five pocket watches, which suggests some relationship to time of which we ought to know the significance: that he was especially prompt, aware of history, afraid of old age, cautious, driven. More likely it represents a love of gadgets. Five watches, two antiques that might have belonged to Grandpa Lawrence or Uncle

Art, one stop watch of some cheap weightless miracle metal, one never-used Westclox still in its box; and—the only one I care about—a silver disc so flat that it reminds me of the dollar pancakes mom used to flap on the griddle.

However, that is also the only watch Bud wants. He wants to buy a silver chain for it and take it home to his wife Michelle. And, after all, the two antiques will go to my progeny, who are boys.

"Remember that old pancake griddle we used to have?"

"Yes, why?"

"I wonder what happened to it."

We sit on the mint-green floor, Bud cross-legged and me with my legs crooked to one side although I am fifty and he is fifty-four, and we don't often sit this way any more. It has something to do with being siblings, children. It has something to do with being orphans. He is bald and black-bearded, he used to amuse my boys and his girls by saying that his hair had melted and slid down his chin. He is loose and lean in the shoulders and thickening at the waist, heading for pear-shaped, like dad.

But Bud was four when I was born, and so I see all his ages layered in him, and of these the thickening middle-aged man before me is the least real. He is still, as I am to myself, a child to me. I see him barely teen-age, forelock dipped over his eye in a black curl, a yellow pencil stub behind his ear, cool nerd, already sardonic, the journalist. Whereas Dad, being grown when I came into the world, is in my memory a single and continuous self.

Our father's body was soft and loose; his upper arms jiggled when he ran. In summer in the swimming pools he wore blue twill boxer trunks with the string hanging out. He hitched the suit up over his girth. He had saggy breasts and a loose broad belly that hung forward to hold up his trunks. He was not much concerned with fat but didn't like to be chided for it. There was dark hair neither thick nor sparse over his chest and down his arms. I found this apparition mildly but only mildly embarrassing, because it meant old man, a person of father-age. My father's body was never otherwise, was never trim or muscular or more or less wrinkled than I remember it at the pools—vast and crowded Encanto, or intimate and shabby El Vista, or Martinez's south of town, where a real stream, cold from underground, ran through a wire fence and into the slimy slanted side of the pool. That place was always full of a nervous mix of skin colors, these being also present in my mother's voice in the words "South Central." There Dad and I stood under a waterfall and froze to the bone, the purpose being then to fling ourselves back out on the bank in the baking sun. And these swimming sessions continued, did they not, into my teen years, into my adulthood whenever I came home? They seem to belong to the easy swing of childhood, but I remember, once, driving south on Central, telling Dad about being hopelessly in love with an unavailable man, so surely they never really stopped? There was, perhaps, a period after I was eleven that they stopped?

"Look at these."

There are bundles of pencils, charcoal, Eagle, Eberhardt, Castell, bound in rubber bands like firewood faggots. There are boxes of new Pink Pearl erasers, of which he never let the supply dwindle. There are templates in translucent green, translucent amber, silver metal; a series of neon orange triangles, two sets of German drafting tools in their velvet-lined boxes, which we remember precisely because they were kept so carefully locked away. There's also a single French curve of clouded plastic—called French but suggesting something more exotic, Oriental, a peacock or paisley, and representing every possible shape, proportion, and variation on the curve known to architecture. Neither Bud nor I can use this mysterious tool, but both of us want it and are hesitant to say so. It falls to me for no better reason than that it comes after the watch and Bud commandeered the watch.

These were the tools and whatsits of his trades. He was a plasterer first, before either of us was born, then a machinist, a brickmason, carpenter, contractor, a tool and die maker, a home designer, an architect without a license. During World War II he put airplane wings together, and in the age of missiles he polished missile parts. He invented a spacer for glass bricks, a house number that attracted and refracted light, a toy propeller, a parking tower for trailers so that low-income transients with a taste for culture like himself would have cheap access to a city. He liked signs and advertising. He kept an ear out for slogans, jingles. He took an interest in the atom.

"Remember this?"

It's an address book, or rather not a book at all but a hinged flat metal box with an arrow that zips down the alphabet printed on the side. You set the arrow and push a lever; the top flips up to reveal . . . now, at the letter C, the words *cupboard, closet, circuit, counter, cost, construction, ceiling,* and, set apart below, *kitchen* with the *k* double-underlined, in case he looked for it on the wrong page.

He was dyslexic, though none of us heard that term until his middle age, and it was not applied to him till he was in his seventies. Up to then he just was a rotten speller. He could draft a house design to scale with an eye so true it hardly needed a ruler to it, but he spelled *linen* with two n's and *closet* with an *it*. Mom made him the spelling kit of the words he needed, the one-syllable pitfalls: den, porch, sill; and the confounding illogic English multisyllabism: masonite, bathtub, piping, quarter-inch, foundation.

"Do you want it?"

"What would I do with it? But otherwise . . . well, okay, yes."

There are paper clips and spring clips, staples, connectors of every sort, but nothing to connect. A paper punch and boxes of little reinforcement rings. There are a half-dozen blotters, blue ink-sopped on the back and on the front a miniature calendar of the month, the name of Del Webb Supply, and a picture of a golden babe, this one in a red velvet skating rig, that one in wisps of blue sunsuit, another as a waitress in roller skates. All their skirts skim rounded buns, the cheeks like peaches. All their breasts are globes with buttons. What is to be done with them? There was so little prurience in him that to have had three Petti calendars in his drawer was proof of—what? That he was in the building trade.

There are tie tacks in the form of airplanes studded with semi-precious stones, initialed cufflinks, mother-of-pearl collar studs, and a bolo tie with a kachina slide. Dad liked to think of himself as dapper, and in later years he came to adorn himself in decorator colors. When he was no longer building he would wear maroon jackets and morning glory ties, lime polyester trousers with lemon shirts, baby-blue Monkey Ward tattersall with ultramarine cuffed duck, pink shirts with painted ties. His color was still good.

There are coins in jars and purses, pennies in scrubbed-out shoe polish tins, nickels in mint boxes, a whole former mayonnaise pint in quarters. My father always checked the edge of dimes and quarters for a copper strip. He had a collection of several hundred dollars' worth that were pure silver. But that he sold, for silver weight, at the handsome profit of six hundred dollars which he then invested in a Broadway show that flopped. These coins are ordinary chicken feed, the silver layered with copper, and not enough to seem worthwhile, qua change.

After Mom died, there was a period when Dad called me late at night. "Can anyone be listening to this?" he'd say. "Is it possible your phone is tapped?"

"Dad, why would anyone tap my phone?"

"Don't tell anybody. Buy silver."

"What?"

"Are you putting your money into silver bars?"

"Dad, I'm putting my money into corn flakes. I don't have any to invest."

"Set some aside. Buy silver."

"Why?"

"America is going to have a depression, it's going to make the thirties look like a piece of cake."

This went on maybe twice a week for a couple of months and then it stopped. When I told Marjie about it, she said, "Oh! See? He can't allow himself to have depression, no one of that generation can. So America's going to have it for him."

My reaction to this was relief and gratitude. It made sense to me. It made metaphoric sense, it was not craziness, it was a coping mechanism. Anyone can tell you: even nuts is functional if it's a coping mechanism.

There's a coping saw. A hacksaw, four packets of new blades. Why is this what's left us? A set of spark plugs. A distributor cap. An automotive coil of some sort neither of us recognizes.

"No," Bud says. "It's for a boat, part of an outboard. I don't know how I know."

We lived in the desert but Bud and I both remember Dad best at water's edge. We remember him launching a sailboat, dragging a canoe off the stony beach, always in some version or other of the twill trunks over which his belly hung in a pale parabola.

We went to Balboa and Laguna and rented sailboats for more per hour than he made per hour. We went to Banff and took pictures of ourselves in a canoe against the glaciers and the glacial sky. We rode a speedboat over the surf from Catalina, bucking waves as hard as boards. Dad built a motor boat and we took it to Lake Apache where we caught, one after another, luminous yellow perch just barely big enough to eat. We took a trailer to Seal Beach and set it up beside the channel, where Dad worked through the summer, designing houses on a board set aslant over the tiny sink while Bud and I stabbed crabs on the channel rocks with a nail-on-the-end pole and walked under the highway in a tunnel riven by a trickle of dirty water.

He went to Alaska after we were too old to vacation with him and Mom any more, and there invented his famous (to us) and still-feasible (why not?) "Car-go Boat," an aluminum flat barge so light it could be pulled by a Volkswagen Bug, and powered by the axle of the car once you got to water and drove aboard her.

When he died the garage was filled with a canoe, long plastic tubes he was gluing or laminating to the sides—in a mistaken (we believe) belief that he could make the airflow lift the boat above the water's friction. The boat was ruined but the Boy Scouts took it anyway.

And he who so loved the ocean is now to go into it. The Neptune Society will drop his ashes off a sailboat between Long Beach and Catalina. Except that they have apparently mislaid the ashes.

Our father's body is in transit from A.L. Moore and Sons of Phoenix to the Neptune Society in Los Angeles, who will scatter him into the sea where he most often chose to be when he had a choice. We didn't have him embalmed, and the casket that went for cremation was some kind of composition essentially cardboard. It was what he wanted, cremation and least possible fuss. We did not dispatch our father's body in a cardboard box in order to save money, though of course there is a residual guilt, as if we had. In those days after his death I thought involuntarily and often of cremation, and once I dreamed of it. I had heard somewhere that body fat rises to the surface. When I dreamed his burning, I saw his body as it used to be, not the paper husk of him that died but the soft swimmer, the fleshy pear. I saw him blister.

We sent him to the fire in a cardboard box, and here we have what's left in a cardboard box. There are jars of keys. We spill them on the rug. Skeleton keys and house keys, car keys from makes of car we know he owned and from makes we know he didn't. Suitcase and briefcase keys, though he never had a briefcase; old and gold, tiny and light keys, a pair that are etched with filigree, a dozen Masterlock, padlock and locker keys. Keys to nothing. There are a few we have dealt with before, deposit box keys that we thought would solve the riddle of the garbled will, so baffling in its combination of legalese and faulty grammar, clearly specifying what to do if this or that beneficiary predeceased another, but not specifying what went to whom if Bud and Gladys and I were all, as we are, living. But there was no deposit box and these were keys to nothing.

There is a wide translucent loop of red celluloid, scored around its circumference about three quarters of the way across. We both recognize it at the same moment: it's a band from the dictaphone that dad had when we were—what?—in fourth and eighth grades, and he had decided to write essays on topics humorous and scientific. If we could find a dictaphone circa 1945, we could hear his voice; we could learn at least what he had wanted, then, to be heard, when later he wanted so little, and then nothing, to escape his mouth.

When I was five and six I sat in his lap facing the radio as if it were a fire; and he told his youth, how he learned to drive a motor car from a book because he was not allowed to touch the wheel, how he became mechanic to the Boy Scouts and got to travel free, to Louisiana, Sault Ste. Marie, Yellowstone. My Dad could remember what went wrong with each of those Boy Scout touring cars, the mis-wiring of the Model T in '22, the radiator leak in the '29 Pierce Arrow. He could talk a blue streak, he could get on a jag and go with it: the way a distributor distributes, the plot of a movie, a new plastering swirl technique, the chronology of a trip and what he saw on it, stalactites, the mother bear, the mud geyser, the redwood with a girth of ninety feet. One night Bud asked him about the cars he'd owned, and Dad went through all forty-five in order, the dates he bought them, the year, model and condition of each, the price he paid and the price he got when he moved onto the next.

He loved the theater, radio, the movies, Charles Wesley's hymns, Ken Murray's Blackouts, Ziegfield's Follies. "My Friend Irma," "My Friend Flicka." He liked to be read to, he liked to hear "pieces," he took us to Hollywood to stand in line for free tickets to "Stella Dallas." He wanted stories, skits, elocution, anecdotes, the news, a shaggy dog.

But after Mom died he quieted, and over the eleven years with Gladys he spoke less and less. When the cancer took him, the voice went first. In hospital he scarcely spoke at all. *Yes, no. I guess so. So you say.* I wanted to shout at him, shake him. "Don't you realize this is our last chance?" But I didn't need anyone to tell me that it was his death and he was allowed to conduct it as he chose.

I flew back and forth to Arizona six times for his death. On the penultimate trip I asked if he got discouraged, and he answered that question.

"Oh, yes, I lie here at night. If I had a way to kill myself I would."

He said this with an inflection that made it clear he expected me to be shocked. When I said, "I know," he picked up his head from the pillow an inch or so. "If I could get some of that stuff. I can't remember the name."

I knew what he meant. One of his old stories, a favorite, was about the time in Bowie in the early thirties, when he was working in the grocery store, that he sold a drinking glass to a man who drank poison from it that night in his hotel room.

"Cyanide," I said.

"Yes. If I knew how to get some of that. . . ."

It was a question, a request. I sat thinking of the consummate innocence of a man who, in 1987, would think of cyanide; the implied content of a man who hadn't followed the fashions in suicide for sixty years.

"I'm sorry you have to go through that sort of discouragement, Dad," I said. He took this for the refusal that it was, and retreated into silence.

Later I told Marjie the curious circumstance of Dad's lymphoma, that it manifested in the roof of his mouth although there are no lymph nodes in the mouth. Marjie said, "Oh, my God. Of course." She meant that he would not open his mouth to let the poison out.

Three years from now I will read that it is a peculiar modern form of self-righteousness to blame the cancerous for their cancers in this was.

"What's this?"

Here is *Machinery's Handbook, Eleventh Edition,* 1942, published by the Industrial Press and according to the title page distributed in Britain from a War-Time Address of 17 Marine Parade, Brighton. The machinists' tools have gone to auction, their sleek oak box is on its way to my home to hold jewelry on the green felt floors of its long flat drawers; but I did not know what to do with the book, covered in malleable leather, three inches thick and indexed with black and gilt tabs like that other bible. I open it at random, show Bud a table of "Feeds for Box tools," divided into *roughing* and *finishing* from 1/16th to 5/8ths *diameter of stock*, and specifying the *brass rod, machine steel* and *tool steel feed per revolution*. The table is precise to within thousandths of an inch. What it means to me is: nothing. I know roughly what "rough" and "finish" mean. I have generic concepts for feed, box, and steel. Here is exactitude, its clues and symbols, and I am illiterate. What shall we do with it? It is out of date; no one who would understand it would now find it useful. I will take it home, I will put it back in the center slot of the tool box whence it came, among the alien imprecision of earrings and African beads.

I'm illiterate in so many signs. There's so much that I can't operate or read, memories that don't explain or fit, that make no more useful legacy than another thingmabob in the cardboard box.

This one, for instance, a memory slightly distorted, as the memory of a place is distorted by the photographs that remain of having visited it: I think this took place when I was in sixth grade, my eleventh year. What I now recall is that Mom was dressing for a PTA meeting, putting on her powder and running a comb through her hair, and I lay down on the double bed to chat to her while she dressed. Dad came in and lay down beside me, we all talked, and then she left. He began to tell me a story—memory makes it the one about the log that they tied on the back of the Ford with the shot brakes to drive it down the mountain at Yellowstone. I don't know if this is right. What is clear in my mind is that I was getting sleepy, and that he reached across with his right hand and put it on my nub of left breast, began to squeeze, a little half-laugh in his throat as he carried on with the story, my skin working in his fist. What I remember best is the stinging of my ears, my heart crashing under his hand, part fear, part disbelief. I remember that what I thought came hammering clear and slow: *This has never happened before. No father has ever done this. This is the worst thing that has ever happened in the world.*

Later Marjie will ask me to draw the scene, and when I do, it will be the view from over my left shoulder, looking down onto the bed, the two heads, two bodies, four legs, his hand across my body. "Funny," I'll say, "I've drawn myself without arms or a mouth."

"Of course. How would you defend yourself?"

And this seems right to me, revelatory, neat as a pin.

I don't remember what I did. Memory is numb, as that breast has been without feeling forty years. It never happened again. I remember that afterward I nursed this terrible secret with great self-pity and a sense of apocalypse; that the daily events of home which took on again the same pattern of familiar dullness would suddenly reverse and reveal themselves to me as a terrible lie. I remember that I pitied and disdained my mother, and also that most of the time I forgot about it. I remember that in college I looked back, wise and cool, thinking: *well, they've always told me I was given to melodrama.* I remember thinking both that it was the end of the world and that I had made too much of it in my mind. I don't remember when I first heard of incest or abuse as a possible human phenomenon. I don't remember when I learned how much worse it could be, or how apocalyptic it always was. It was not a major subject then, as it became. It didn't seem to anyone to explain a life.

Now Bud and I sit surrounded with the debris, and it has to remind us both of Christmas, the gifts denuded of their wrappings and diminished into little piles.

"No toothbrush," Bud says. "Our Dad raised good-natured kids."

I agree. Darwin said that animals make noise in order to augment whatever feeling is necessary at the time: a dog growls to make itself ferocious, and a cat hisses to be dangerous. Soldiers joke going into battle because pretending to feel brave can make you brave. Now Bud and I praise each other, how generous we have been to each other over our father's death. It makes us helpful to say we are so. It makes us love each other more to say we do.

Marjie will say, "Why can't you get angry? Really you are, deeply, angry!"

And maybe she's right. But it doesn't feel like something too deep to feel. It seems to me that what I think is also what I feel: that this was a man so innocent it never crossed his mind—no, rather, that he felt some guilt but was able in the moment's impulse to rationalize it, and that later he put it out of mind.

"No man can do that! He knew what he was doing!"

No doubt she's right. I can't be so innocent as to believe he was innocent, can I?

But it continues stubbornly to seem: that he did something awful not meaning to, and forgot it after. There's so much evidence around. There's so much stuff here, keys to nothing, staples, paper clips.

My friend Mose will tell me, oh, a matter of years from now, about the moment of death of his cat Max. At the moment of death, he will say, Max seemed to shrink; there was a sudden, subtle diminishing. And Mose could see how the notion came about, of the spirit leaving the body. He could see that something seemed to disperse itself invisibly into space. Then I will think of Dad, the skin shrunk over his bones, how I felt nothing, and also felt that it was not he; how he was dispersed into memory, past knowing, beyond judgment.

Here's another tie tack, this one in the form of a turbine engine.

A spring weight with a hook.

Foreign coins from countries he never visited: Italy, France, a set of six Imperial dollars intended for the occupation of America by Japan. An English sixpence, from the one "foreign" country he did get to. In a hardwood frame, a collection of Republican campaign buttons mounted on red felt. I like Ike. Win with Nixon. Elect Dewey. Among seven children and grandchildren he could claim one Republican. What will we do with these?

Bud calls the Neptune Society, but the ashes have not arrived.

THE DEATH OF
THE FATHERS

DOLORES SCHWARTZ

AS I STARE AT my bookshelf trying to decide how to begin writing about my father's death, I am caught by a massive volume called *World of Our Fathers*. It is about the world of Eastern European Jews and their lives in America. The title, of course, recognizes only the fathers, as so often happens. And, as always, it is a short step from macro- to microcosm.

In the little world in which I grew up, I had a mother, but I never questioned that my father ruled, and his rule was, by and large—but not totally—harsh. His was no iron hand in a velvet glove; there was no glove at all.

And yet.

My feelings about my father can, most accurately, be termed ambivalent. Certainly, there were times when all I felt for him was hate. I wanted him dead for years, even before he died in 1976 at the age of 84. There were times when my magically-inclined child's mind believed I could make him die.

For most of my childhood he was psychologically absent. He worked hard during the day, and at night ranted and raved at me, the oldest and most rebellious of his three children.

When I was eleven, he had a heart attack, brought on, my mother said, by my having "aggravated" him. All I remember is watching orderlies load him onto a stretcher, then carry him to the ambulance waiting outside. To my mother he said, "It's been nice knowing you." To me, he said nothing.

My father recovered and lived almost thirty more years. He never had another heart attack, but the threat of one was used to keep me in line. I argued with him about everything, especially when I was a teen-ager. For example, when I was brash enough to say that I didn't want to get married, didn't think I wanted to have children (a sentiment that was nearly unthinkable in the 1950s), he told me, "Don't talk crazy. You're not normal." Whenever I tried to explain my thoughts, my father withdrew to take a nap or he laughed at me. It is that mocking laughter that rings in my ears today. As an adult, I still have difficulty determining if people are laughing with me or at me— or if they are laughing at all.

My family, relatives, and many of my friends say my father was a gentle, quiet man, struggling to make ends meet in an often-cruel world. I saw him as a tyrant, someone who was comfortably at home in cruelty. Neither I nor my sisters could do anything without his agreement, which he generally withheld. For he had rules, and he expected his wife and children to obey them.

Rule One: Never trust anyone who is not a blood relative—and some of those are suspect, too.

Rule Two: Do not tell secrets to children, whatever their ages. At 19, I learned accidentally that he had been married before, certainly no cause for either secrecy or condemnation. But it made me wonder what other secrets lurked for me or someone else to uncover accidentally.

Rule Three: Never trust anyone who is not Jewish. (This rule greatly restricted my social life as I grew up. We did not live in a Jewish neighborhood, and I attended elementary and junior high schools where I was one of only two Jews.)

Rule Four: Don't argue with your father or cross him in any way. Otherwise, he would have a heart attack or leave and go to his mother. (At the slightest argument he was off to my grandmother's; when she died, he threatened to kill himself.)

They are all truths, these rules, about the way my father lived his life, and expected us to live ours. But they aren't the only truths in our family. If they were, this story would be simpler to understand, just as it would have been easier to live through.

*****

I cannot discount my other fathers—the many faces of this one man. In my baby book there are poems that one of them wrote to me, tender poems by a man who did not think his baby was at all crazy or abnormal.

Another father took me to birthday parties because I was painfully shy and refused to go without him. I wanted my father's presence more than my mother's, so whenever I was invited somewhere, he took time off to hold my hand and tell me there was nothing to fear.

As I grew older, *he* became more afraid as he saw me leaving home both physically and psychologically. He must have felt helpless when it came to convincing me that the world was a dangerous place.

But there came a point when my father's efforts to control me and my behavior no longer worked. After I graduated from college, I chose to live in another city thousands of miles from my home town.

When my father came to visit me in my basement apartment, he tried to bribe the superintendent (who lived across the hall) to rig an alarm that would sound in his apartment if I got "in trouble." I refused.

Today, yet another father enters my field of vision. I know he existed, although I am only now beginning to fully trust the visual flashbacks that tell me so. This is the man who took naps with his four-year-old daughter in the same bed where he slept with his wife. This is the man who fondled that daughter, touched her between her legs, and put her hand on his penis. This is the man who said, "Don't tell."

All of these faces were my father's, and some days I find the sum of them too volatile to contemplate if I wish to function in the world. I am not happy with this multi-faceted vision, because I cannot create a whole, unfragmented picture from it. Not yet.

*****

I last saw my father alive about two days before he died. He was sitting in an ornately carved rocking chair near the front door of my parents' house, waiting for my mother to take him to a doctor's appointment.

"How do you feel?" I asked. "Are you going somewhere?"

He laughed, cackled actually, one of his mocking laughs, and said, "I'm all right. I'm on my way to a Chinese dinner party."

Two nights later my husband, two friends, and I were having a late dinner in a restaurant when we received the message that he had died. My mother had located us through our babysitter, and she delivered the message calmly.

After eating dinner my father had gone to take a nap in the same bedroom where he once napped with me. When my mother went to check on him an hour or so later, he was, as she put it, "gone."

Our friends drove us to my parents' house, and then went to break the news to our children, staying with them until we could return home.

My mother told me I could—or did she say *should?*—go into the bedroom to "say good-bye" to my father. I could not move my legs and did not know why. My husband gently prodded me in the direction of the room where he lay.

I hadn't been in that bedroom for years. It seemed crowded with too much furniture, and the double bed appeared small and narrow, too small for my father's five-foot-nine-inch height. It made me think of the beds in European hotels, sleeping shells seemingly made for people who flourished before this era of multi-vitamins.

Looking hard, I tried to intuit some message on his face, but saw none. I felt nothing. I looked inside myself for a final farewell. Again, nothing—which was close to what I had received from him when he was alive. Somehow, *nothing* was an appropriate response on both our parts. The only difference between us was that he was dead and I was alive.

But there was no sense of hatred. His violation had left me too numb for that. I did, however, have the sense that at last I would become close to my mother, since she would no longer have to intercede between us. Unfortunately, that hasn't happened, the reasons for which are a different story altogether.

I have never grieved for my father, though I know I must someday. And I know that grief will be for the father I did not have as well as for the ones whose presences seemed to contradict each other. It is so hard to know which ones were real, which ones I may have imagined—and why. And which ones were poses of a man who, like many others of his era, simply did not know how else to make his way in the world.

Seventeen years is a long time not to mourn. I have tried to understand my refusal. I have also puzzled over his "Chinese dinner party." Why Chinese? And why a dinner party?

The times of which I've written weren't the best of times, but they weren't the worst of times either. I suffered other abuse in my family, worse than that at my father's hands. But I also know there are many people in the world whose suffering is far greater than mine.

All I can say is that self-disgust and shame die hard, a harder death than my father's. That is why, in writing this essay, I am using a pseudonym to hide my identity. I will continue to do so until I have mourned, not only the death of my fathers, but also the four-year-old little girl who still lives inside me because she is not ready to die—or do I mean, *to live?* She deserves survival.

JOURNEY

ANDREA CHAPIN

Durham, New Hampshire

IT IS THE NIGHT before my father's memorial service. We are together again in the large, rambling house where we grew up. Until the last few months of his life my father was always moving, talking and drinking, a flurry of activity and words. And though he's not here with us, we are his children, and when together the five of us manage to become a flurry of activity, too, all talking at the same time, a loud machine of constant motion with cogs and pistons and steam.

My sisters' children run through the rooms in their pajamas laughing, crying, never quiet. My eldest brother Teddy wanders from the kitchen, where he's been fixing himself Perfect Manhattans all night, through the living room—where his boyfriend and my boyfriend are watching an animated children's video on TV—to the downstairs bedroom. As he bursts through the bedroom door, metal coat hangers crash to the floor with a tinny clatter. He waves his hands in the air.

I am on the bed with my two sisters. With a green steno pad in my hand, I am trying to reread the piece about my father I wrote one sunny afternoon in Montana, two weeks before I found out he had cancer.

Flathead Lake, Montana

My father is a big, broad man. He's not unusually tall, but he has big hands and big feet and a chest and girth that have thickened over the years, not into flab but into a strong, dense mass that towers. He's not tall, not even six feet. But he walks big, very big. And he walks a lot, always moving. And he likes to work with his hands, lifting things and carrying them, always opening something or shutting it, fixing a hose or a hinge, drilling holes, nailing something or screwing it.

And when he screws a screw, simple you'd think, with a screwdriver and a hole. But he takes his two hands, paws really, and takes hold of that screwdriver and twists, not just with his wrists, but with his whole body, all the energy he can find, all the way up from the toes of his big feet, and screws that screw as if his whole life, and everybody else's, depended upon it, hunching his shoulders and making every muscle taut. And the screw, once so small, becomes something huge, something he's battling with, a big powerful force he has to conquer, tame.

And then it's done, screwhead flush to the surface. But he can't leave it at that. He has to place the blade of the screwdriver back into the lip of the screw and again, with every cell of power he can muster, turn the screw, just to make sure it's really in there, just to make sure it won't move, just to make sure he gave it everything, gave it his all.

Now, almost two years later, my words seem to carry an eerie premonition, a final glimpse of him before the disease set in, a parting shot. I will read this piece tomorrow at his memorial service, and I am trying to practice tonight, trying to make it past the third line. It describes my father's relentless energy, his restlessness that has finally come to rest. What it doesn't mention is the evenings when he sucked down vodka as if it were ice water, the days when he sipped Bloody Marys from morning 'til night—as if all the lifting and carrying, the opening and shutting, the drilling and nailing and struggling created within him an unquenchable thirst.

My eldest sister Alexandra is lying on her side in a crisp red silk dress with a pad of white paper. She shakes her head. I just don't know what to say, she says with pencil poised ready to catch what she cannot think of. Can't I just read yours? I always do this, she says, pulling the pencil away, taking a sip of Scotch from the glass she's been balancing on her knee.

Every time my middle sister Nessa hears a noise coming from the baby walkie talkie she carries around with her she runs out of the room. She's back now and has spread herself out on the bed. She still hasn't decided what to read either, maybe a passage from a letter, but she'll burst into tears, she says, she knows she will.

My middle brother David, with a straight, let's-get-down-to-business face, charges back and forth between the rooms with his cheerful, smiling, blond, second-wife-to-be in tow. He is the self-appointed organizer, he is the coach with the play at hand but he cannot seem to get his players to stay in a huddle. He is orchestrating, deciding that we need to input everything we are going to say tomorrow on his portable computer. He sets the computer up in the living room. I give presentations all the time, he says, that's my job. You have to have a program.

My mother is in the living room sitting in a chair that seems too big for her; her legs don't touch the ground. She's five foot one and when she stands next to us she looks like a plump, silver-haired elf. Her children tower over her, just as her husband did.

Fort Myers, Florida

And now, it is my father with his two large-boned hands on my shoulders. We are waiting in the car while my mother signs in. He is lying in the back seat, on his side, curled in a fetal position, waiting, in the air conditioning, as I am waiting, listening to the sandpaper sounds of his breathing. Then I pull him to his feet, the way I've pulled him to his feet fifty, maybe a hundred times before, when he was too drunk to stand, when I had to help him up from where he'd fallen, guide him up the creaking stairs.

Today his large frame is gaunt and teetering, his face a mask of sickness. But I do it. I manage to get him standing and now we're walking, inches at a time. He's shuffling, using me like one of those metal-framed walkers, both hands pressing down hard on my shoulders. My father is not old, but he is dying and now moves like a man of ninety, maybe a hundred. And it takes us forever to make it to the hospital door.

As we sisters wander into the living room to rehearse what we are going to say the next day, my two brothers have embarked upon another project and are now in the kitchen putting my father's ashes in a blue glazed vase, shaped like an urn, that Teddy made years ago on a potter's wheel. My mother remains in the living room, while we crowd into the kitchen. There is an unspoken feeling of fascination, unreality—how can a man once so big fit into a container the size of a paint can? It truly seems impossible. Where has he gone? The kitchen table is covered with newspapers and on it sits the vase. David takes a screwdriver and pries open the metal container; Teddy drunkenly holds the vase to the table as David pours. I expect to see gray dust, but the ashes are ivory colored and look like sediment— pieces of shell and fossil you'd find embedded in rock. I have the urge to dig my fingers into the coarse rubble and let the pieces run through my hand like sand, in the hopes of finding a tooth, or a shape of bone I'd recognize. But there is nothing distinguishable, nothing, really, of him left in there.

By some miracle, the ashes fit perfectly into the vase. David, with fierce precision, prepares the epoxy in the kitchen sink, measuring, stirring, mirroring my father who mixed epoxy year after year to fix a broken this, an unhinged that. Teddy unveils his prize—a circular copper plaque to affix to the top of the vase. Earlier, he found a blacksmith in a neighboring town who cut the plaque from a copper plate my father had proudly brought back from a business trip; my father's name is now engraved on it with the dates 1926–1990. Before my brothers seal the vase, Teddy reaches in and grabs a handful of the ashes and puts them in a plastic sandwich bag. By this time his mind is reeling with alcohol, and he jokes as he puts the plastic bag in his breast pocket, "This is for my cereal tomorrow morning."

We sort of laugh and sort of think it's weird, but everything about death and dying seems weird to us. Teddy doesn't mix the ashes with his cereal in the morning but places the little plastic bag in my father's closet in the living room—a sacred place that for years housed all the things that were important to my father: boxes of slides and home movies; the shrapnel taken from his legs when he was eighteen and the ambulance he was driving in Italy was bombed; the autobiographical essay "Belsen: Synonym for Hell"—about his experiences evacuating the Belsen concentration camp at the end of the war—that was published in a Montana literary review called *Mountaineer*; his philosophy papers from college; photographs of his father, who wrote an amazing journal while working in a bank in China at the age of seventeen, who died at the age of twenty-seven (my father was four) when the plane he was flying crashed in Red Bank, New Jersey. My grandfather lived a fast-paced, flamboyant, roaring-twenties life of investment schemes and penthouse apartments, yachts, private planes and fancy cars—all of which came crashing down with his plane and the stock market.

Teddy says he put the baggie of my father's ashes in the closet so that my father would always be in the house, but Teddy never tells anyone and months later my mother cleans out the closet. One day Teddy calls and mentions the baggie to her, and as is typical with our family, she doesn't tell him what she's done but gets off the phone, bursts into tears, and calls me—because the closet is already cleaned and days ago when she first started the project she unknowingly threw the little bag of ashes out.

The morning of the memorial service, in a family ritual of our own creation—the only type our atheistic father would have wanted—my two brothers pull from the lawn the large round flat rock, a giant's skipping stone, my father brought from a stream bed somewhere years ago because he liked its shape. As my father requested, we dig a hole and put the blue glazed vase in the hole and cover it with dirt and replace the large stone and feel that he, our father, is now under us and around us, spreading through the earth and the air.

Around noon in the hot, end-of-summer sun, seventy people assemble on the lawn: relatives, friends from town, university students that rented rooms and apartments in our house, business associates, and the carpenter, electrician, tile man, and plumber who worked on our house over the years and became my father's friends. We play Beethoven's *Eroika*, his favorite symphony, and say our pieces: how our father loved his family, put his family before his own happiness or success, lived by a principle he called the Big *R*: Responsibility to his family—something that he saw as a virtue but I see as a curse, a scarlet letter, an albatross, he wore throughout his conflicted life, preventing him from being responsible first to himself.

And we read our poems. "*I am the captain of my ship,*" David

reads from one of my father's favorite Robinson Jeffers's poems. "*I am
the captain of my ship. . . .*" the line seems suspended in the stagnant
August air. I marvel at the way my father loved his children—a love
he found easier to express as he got older—but not himself; the way
he shared with us the small things in life that filled him with glee—a
smooth stone, an old coin, a bug on a leaf, a piece of wood; the way
he constantly wrote little notes to the five of us—once a week, twice a
week, we got letters from him with an interesting magazine article, a
newspaper clipping; the way his boundless curiosity kept him
questioning and discovering while his fears often paralyzed him; the
way his blue eyes lit up when he smiled and laughed; the way he
professed the importance of being responsible yet became completely
irresponsible in his drunkenness night after night, year after year.

On the lawn under the sun, we continue only with our public
memories: how our father had a good sense of humor and loved to
tell stories; how he had a sense of humor even about his death and
dying; how when he found out he was terminally ill with lung cancer
six months after he had retired from the job he had (and hated, but
we don't mention this) in a small wire and cable factory for over thirty
years, he decided not to take any treatment but to do what he had
always wanted to do which was travel, until he was too sick, travel
and take his children with him. And Nessa does, as she said she
would, burst into tears while she is reading a letter and Alexandra has
to finish reading it for her.

But ghosts come out at night, and when the people have all gone
home and the sun has set, my brother Teddy, thirty-eight, the eldest
son, the gay son, the son who—for the first twenty years of his life—
battled with a father who all too often seemed to hate him and then
who nursed that father through a nervous breakdown, starts sounding
more and more, in words, phrases, even whole sentences, like my
father when he was drunk and cruel, verbally attacking the same

people my father had—David's ex-wife, Aunt Helen. Finally, in an eerie awful scene, as we sit in the living room Teddy starts to attack my mother; we can hear my father's voice now coming out of my brother's mouth, and we are horrified and remember too clearly, too painfully, all the nights as children when we would wake up to the sound of that same voice screaming. Sometimes the walls and floors seemed as thin as paper. My mother shrieking at my father. My father thundering back at her. The anger and rage seemed to blow into our rooms from below and hang there, keeping us awake and listening.

During his life, drinking let my father's rage surface, and when the alcohol ran through his system he raged against his job, against people with money and success, against my mother, against his children. I suppose he raged the least against me because I was the youngest, the baby of the family, and somehow I learned early on to rage back at him, to scream at him for drunken episodes, to empty all the bottles of alcohol in the sink in futile, desperate attempts to stop his drinking. The saddest rage of all was his anger at his father. He was so young when his father died, and he felt cheated that he had never known this man, great in his eyes. I remember nights, long ago now, when my father would raise his clenched fist in the air, shake it and yell at his father for dying, the son-of-a-bitch dying, a grown man screaming at his father's ghost.

And this night plays itself out in much the same way those nights did as we got older and tried to intervene. Alexandra is with her in-laws. David is driving someone home, but the rest of us fall into our accustomed roles. My mother runs out of the house, crying. My sister Nessa tells me to run after our mother and I do and I find her, a seventy-year-old woman, sitting on the picnic table in the back, sobbing under the stars.

New York, New York

I dream I had recently: I am going to a cocktail party in a large, modern suburban house somewhere. I am walking down the path that leads to the front door. It's a summer evening, still light. The grass in the yard is a dark rich green. A man wearing a light blue polo shirt and charcoal colored slacks is a few paces in front of me. He carries himself with ease; his shoulders are relaxed, his gait steady. The man opens the door and turns to let me pass on ahead of him. It is my father. But this version of my father is comfortable with himself, contented; he is tanned and trim, not bloated from drink nor emaciated from illness. All the fury, all the tenseness, all the struggle, have disappeared and what is left is a man who seems pleased with himself, enjoys life, is happy. And as I pass him at the door of this unknown house in this unknown suburb, he smiles at me and I smile back at him.

Apizaco, Mexico

I was in a little town in Mexico called Apizaco. I'd risen early to go to the market. It was cool as I walked, the streets still hidden in shadows. A small boy was walking in front of me with someone leaning on him, an arm placed heavily on his shoulder. At first I thought the figure with the boy was an old woman in baggy bell bottoms, a torn sweater, and a kerchief wrapped around her head. Every step seemed an effort. As they veered off to the left at the fork in the road, I passed them. Leaning on the small boy was a man in his mid thirties—maybe the boy's father. His face was slow, matching his walk, his features heavy with sickness. The weight was in the boy's face, too. What a strong little boy inside and out, I thought, carrying more than this man's weight upon his narrow sloping shoulders.

RIDI, PAGLIACCIO

STEPHANIE S. TOLAN

FLOATING. THAT'S HOW IT seemed to me when I entered your hospital room that bright June morning—that you were floating there, my father, golden and still, King Tut adrift on a morphine sea. You looked as you had looked the night before, except that the white fuzz was gone along your jaw. It must have been Josefina on the morning shift, one of the few who dared to shave you. She had swabbed the blood from your lips, too, and combed your mustache and your soft, newly grown hair. Elegant, you looked, in your still, thin sleep.

Your hands, their long, slim fingers quiet, were crossed on the sheet. The needle that kept you floating, the line that tethered you to the morphine, no longer taped to the bruised arm, led through the hospital's blue-flowered gown directly to your heart.

Sunlight poured through the window, lit the rose I had brought from your yard. I chattered—about the cats, the dog, my breakfast— my voice covering the day's terrible new sound, the wet, alien, bubbling in and out of your breath.

I pulled my chair close, took one hand as gently as I could and began the daily vigil, watching for a frown. The wrinkling of your brow, now so taut against the bone, would mean the pain was cresting, breaking through, that I, your surrogate voice, must call a nurse for more morphine.

I watched your drawn face, waiting for the frown. Knowing it would come. And time slipped sideways, backward.

A blond child stands in the darkness, tears streaming, holding a flashlight unsteadily pointed toward the dirt in front of her—the waste space between garages, weeds, grass, a tangle of shrubbery. A shovel bites downward in the light, a foot against the edge. Hands, movement, thud of dirt, a clattering of stones. And out of the light, unseen, but looming so that the child wishes to drop the light and go to it, cuddle it against the night chill, the small still form of a red-brown dachshund, wrapped in a faded towel. Schatzi. *A sob breaks loose.*

"Stop that crying!" The voice is intense, furious, frightening. "Stop it this minute or I'll send you in and finish this myself!"

The child chokes, bites her lip, tries to steady the light. The tears cannot be stopped, she knows, but he won't see them in the dark. She must only, somehow, find a way to stop their sound. Because she has to be here, has to be part of this ritual, this death, this end. Nine years—all she remembers of her life. How could she not be here to say good-bye? But as with everything, she must earn this right, must be strong enough, even in the darkness of her pain, at the digging of this grave. Stop feeling, stop crying. Be strong. . . .

I was back in the hospital room, staring at your hand in mine, hearing your breath bubbling. Was there ever a time when your message to me was different? When pain was a justification for tears? None I could remember. Tears—even, I suspected, pain—meant failure. Failure of strength, failure of will. What might have been your pain the night Schatzi died, the feeling my childish tears might have set loose from your control? I never knew. I never asked or even wondered. Did you feel that death at all? My mind, in that hospital room, told me you must have, but my memory could not believe it.

The father of my childhood (who was and was not you) was made of iron and stone. He was a giant, a man-figure in a dark suit, in a hat, whose glossy hair and dark mustache were symbols of such difference from me that he could have been a creature from another world. I feared that figure. Wanted to please it, certainly, wanted to earn a smile. But I always knew the frown would come, inevitably. *Because I could not be who I was and meet his demands.* I could not.

Judy and Joey told me I had it easiest—youngest, baby, spoiled. They meant such things as the two-wheeled bike that as a hand-me-down, came earlier for me. Perhaps they were right in other ways. By the time I came along, this father knew a toddler could not sit still for an hour as punishment; he no longer thought prune juice in the face a persuasive disciplinary technique. How they handled his demands I do not know. Perhaps they learned to shut off feeling as Judy learned to stuff a pillow in her mouth to stop the night coughs he did not allow. I did not learn.

I, blond child, youngest, baby, fled to other worlds. Maybe I was looking for the one to which I belonged, the one where I could be myself. The worlds I fled to were found in books. For a long time pirate stories were my favorite: I was Jim, hiding in the apple barrel; I was a cabin boy, the youngest, weakest member of the crew, but the one who survived by wit. Then came the desert island stories. Children stranded on an island, forced to sustain their own lives in their own ways. I read my books, safe in the privacy of my room, in the limbs of the maple, under the black walnut trees—places where every feeling was possible. Where *I* was possible.

Outside of the books I built worlds of imagination, and hundreds of characters to share them. I talked to myself. Followed by ever-changing enemies, I slipped from tree to tree on my way to school, to church, to town. Made treasure maps. Invented the horrifying history of our house, where human teeth marks had been left in a brick set into the basement wall, where mounds beneath the front porch were certain to be graves, where storage closets under the attic eaves had surely once held children, like Sarah Crewe, prisoner. Massive feelings—joy and terror, grief and rage and triumph—were at loose in my world, filling the basement, the attic, the spaces under the bushes where no father ever came.

That father (you and not you) allowed himself anger. Where other feelings showed weakness, anger was strong. It went hand-in-hand with power and control. Judy and Joey grew up and went away, and I felt that anger, power, control focus on me, the one who was left. As childhood's imaginary realms slipped back and out of my grasp, the blond child disappeared from view, her safe places smaller. The pages of my journals. The stories I wrote. The poems.

The feeling self I could not kill lived where and how it could, cloaked itself in doing, winning, writing, living by its wits, climbing the rigging to the very top, a knife between its teeth. And the childhood fear changed to hatred.

When I could, as soon as I could, I packed up what me was left to me and made an island where I could build a life of my own. I thought I had left my father—you, not you, you—behind forever.

But then here I was, forty-nine, this final, sun-filled day, holding a golden hand and watching your face for the frown of pain, remembering. When the chemo worked, your doctor dubbed you Iron Man, little knowing the history that proved it so. It had been iron and stone that kept you caring for the woman you loved beyond your body's power to support your will. But iron and stone could not be all. The hand I held was flesh, as it had always been.

Another memory surfaced, and another—the two I'd kept
sheltered like rare museum exhibits through all the years of fear, all
the years of hatred and distance. Both were memories of what your
hands had made for that blond child.

The Teeny Weeny Camp appeared one spring morning under the
peonies in our backyard in Canton. The white tents, the match-stick-
and fabric cots, the eggshell cauldron over a pebble-ringed fire pit
(scorched like the charred sticks inside, proof that it had been
used)—each detail was perfect. "Shhh," you told me that morning, as
I stared with astonished, all-believing eyes. "They're hiding. If you
make a noise you'll frighten them away."

And sure enough, after my friends had come to share the wonder,
the next day it was all gone. A shred of fabric, a tiny, whittled tent
stake, a bit of broken shell, had been left in their wake as they fled
along a tiny path behind the garage. The Teeny Weenies had been
made as real in their flight as in their coming. Almost I remember
seeing them, bright movement at the corners of my eyes. Judy and
Joey claimed they, too, had had a Teeny Weeny camp once, back in
Dayton, before me. But they could not make my own less special, less
perfect, less real.

From Canton, too, the Halloween shadow box. You made it from
one of your wooden cigar boxes, the lid opening flat to form a corn
field with real, miniature corn shucks, and a jack-o'-lantern, beneath
a full moon carved into the back and covered with yellow paper.
Above flew tiny bats, and a witch on a stick-and-straw broomstick,
suspended on invisible threads in front of the moon. It, too,
was intricate, tiny, perfect. Meant to celebrate Halloween,
it also honored October, the month of my birth. In that way it
celebrated me. I kept it carefully through all the other months so it
could go to school each year. Memory would have it returning
October after October through eons of childhood. But it must

have lasted only till I was eight. It did not get to Wisconsin when we moved.

The two memories. And then a third I did not mean to save, appeared behind them, their dark shadow. Me, a twenty-year-old riding in the car, corn fields rushing by outside, Mother driving me back to school. You (not you) and I had fought ferociously again, both yelling, me no doubt in raging tears, defeated as always.

"Why must you always take him on?" she asked, her eyes on the road. "You force him to take stands against you."

"He doesn't let me breathe, let me *be*. Why can't he ever just support what I want, who I am? What about love? He's my father. Why can't he *love* me?"

"Your father loves you."

A pause. Then her voice so low I had to strain to catch the words, "It's just that he doesn't know how to show it."

A moment to take it in. And then the tears. No attempt to hold them back this time. This, too, was a death, a burial. What use was love not shown? Like food stored, locked away, never offered. I would starve, all the same. Worse, I would starve, had starved my whole life, while on both sides of his wall of iron and stone, was hunger. On both sides pain.

When the tears ended that time, something else had ended with them. Stone the wall was and would remain. Better just to turn away.

And so it was the years of my adulthood. Love walled away on both sides. Gifts, the work of hands and minds, passed back and forth over the top, symbols of what could not come through.

Silver pins, rings, bracelets.

Poems.

Vases, pots, plates.

Books.

And then one autumn day, myself in a car again, the Hudson River rushing by outside, and you, my father, driving. You crying. Crying.

"You don't know, you can't know how it is. Your mother says such terrible things."

"She doesn't mean them. And later she doesn't remember them."

"I remember them."

Alzheimer's. We had the word, now, for what was happening to her, a word too awful for you to hear, too awful for you to say. "The Big A." And feelings, at last, broke through. Such heat melts iron, melts stone. For *this* pain there were tears.

The wall still stood between us, but a hand that day reached through a tiny opening to me. For a moment we touched. And cried together. Then the opening was gone, the stone back in place. "I manage. We manage. We're fine."

Your life, once so full of doing, making, creating, narrowed to caretaking as Mother slipped farther away. Two old people holding hands, leaning together—the photograph hung above my keyboard, looming over my work, until I bashed a hole in your forever wall. "I love you," I wrote at last, old enough to need no answer. "I love you."

Neither you nor I, Father, controlled the force—a husband's job—that brought me home, brought me a thousand miles to a house the two of you could walk to, and finally smashed the wall. Something beyond us was at work, and as a year began with war, I clambered over stone and iron rubble to re-enter your life.

Eight months, we had, of hand touching hand. Then, August, the routine physical, the blood test, the news. "How can it be?" you asked, raising your head from the Merck Manual's lymphoma page. "I feel fine."

Iron and stone.

The last week in May, with Mother in a nursing home and your having moved through and past that pain, those tears, we spoke of death. "Holiday weekend coming up," you said, grinning. "Be done with it. Put me in a balloon—with streamers and confetti. Let me ascend."

"Appropriate," I answered.

"What do *you* think it's like?"

"No one comes back to say. I wish you would. I think it's okay, but I wish you'd let me know for sure. Maybe people can't. Maybe the way a butterfly couldn't explain flight to a caterpillar. Still, I wish—"

And you nodded.

The sun was low in the sky when I slipped out that final day to get my overnight things and to find a box to play the music you could no longer stand through your earphones. "Not long," the doctor had said. "Not long."

And so it was that Caruso sang to both of us near midnight as you took your last breath. "Ridi, Pagliaccio." Laugh, clown. As you would have wanted it. No tears.

And then, in the darkness of that room, through another wall your hand reached back to me. "It's okay. It is."

My father, it is fall again. I moved three day lilies and the rhubarb from your yard to mine today. I do not go willingly to that house, that yard, where I found you and lost you, where I learned we might have been allies all those wasted years in worlds we somehow shared. Teenie Weeny camps and Halloween.

There have been tears. There will be more in a world with such an empty space where once was iron and stone.

Mother, unstuck in time, is the only one of us you have not left. "Josie and I made soup this morning," she tells me. "He's out somewhere now, though. I don't know where. Did you tell him you were coming?"

Maybe you'd be glad to know the walls are down, now, for that blond child, too. She's here with me, laughing, crying, building worlds for both of us. She no longer needs to earn the right to feel, to be. When you reached back that last time to touch me, you set her free. Thank you. We love you.

MY FATHER'S DEATH

MARCIA FALK

Avrom Abba ben Sholom Dovid
may his memory be a blessing

1. After the *shiveh*, at the Metropolitan Museum

Sitting across from Degas'
"Woman with Chrysanthemums,"
spillage of bloom in the center,
on the right, her blasé eye
overscanning the wooden horizon:
Is there a garden there, someone

waiting? In the next room
people coming, leaving (excess
of inscrutable motion, excess
of distraction) pass between
you and the image, where you
thought you would at last find space.

When the crowd thins, wending
toward other attractions,
when it's summer or winter
or a workday or any day,
when you've stopped counting days,
you will try again.

2. Six months later

The world is having a delayed reaction
to my father's death.
Today came a letter of regrets
for not having been there to bury or praise.
As if our actions were a saving grace.

My father floats in a sky of forgetfulness.
Once he asked me to forgive,
now he is easy with himself.
When his hard and heavy breathing
stopped that morning in October,
he had no more expectations.

Let him go, and go on without him.
He is dead and it is late.
Our sins number and multiply
unconsciously, but my father
has no need, forgives all.

Shiveh: In Jewish tradition, the seven-day period of mourning
during which the bereaved receive visitors in their home.

DAD'S DYING

CANDYCE H. STAPEN

To the memory of my father, Jack Homnick

THAT FIRST WINTER. My small daughter methodically piles the bodies one on top of another. Gray limbs fat with dirt protrude in all directions like the pits at Buchenwald. On one, a shiny white shoe dangles below a twisted ankle. On another, tattered blue jeans sway slightly, revealing a dimpled, bloated knee. Another still clutches a velvet green dress, the tiny embroidered heart caught in the curve of fingers. I keep still, sipping my coffee. She drags the last one, almost as big as herself with red matted hair and fixed eyes, its limp body trailing a path in the shag rug to a spot on the floor near the others.

It's done. Wrapped in my sheered velvet robe the color of dried blood, I am the commandant of the morning, silently watching all progress. The sunroom floor is cleared of dolls. Let the day begin.

Like all the other Saturdays, at 9:15 in the morning as I field breakfast requests for omelets and waffles, a phone call burns its way from Hollywood, Florida to Chevy Chase, D.C. "It's Gramma," my three-year-old squeals with delight as she climbs on top of the kitchen counter. I can hear myself stiffen. "Answer it," says my fifteen-year-old in a combination of teen-age questioning and demand.

Wishing to be out jogging with my husband, a middle-aged woman running for her life through rows of shiny Volvos, and Vanagons, I hear the phone's constant ring. Quickly, I throw toasted things at my children, slip into the stone-priest role I've perfected since my father's cancer began, pick up the receiver, and say "Hello, Mom." Judging by her voice, I calculate I have three minutes of pleasantries and polite conversation until she bursts into tears.

"The X-ray report showed no progress. They said that shouldn't have happened. The attacks come more frequently. He can't sleep through the night. He won't take his medicine. Sam, the one he always liked to talk with at the pool last season, just died of a stroke. Dad can't leave the bathroom and there's no one to talk to anyway. I plead with him. I beg him. But he's so depressed. It's bad for me, and worse for him. There's no reason to live, he says. I've never seen him like this. He won't go to Friday night services. He keeps asking why is this happening to him. Cindy's husband, just 32, is dying of leukemia, and she's three months pregnant. "They say he won't live to see the baby. Did you get my birthday card?"

"Yes. Thank you," I say, stalling for answers, trying to know what to address first. "I know this is hard," I say, gesticulating wildly at the cupboard shelf in some mad parody of sign language. My son wants grape jelly. I ignore my daughter who is tormenting the cat again, threading through her long white hair with a dinner fork.

Alissa erupts in screams. The cat, the only one allowed to, scratches back. "Hold on," I order in relief.

Envying the cat's directness, I implore my daughter to speak with

Gramma, hoping a three-year-old won't know I'm really begging. "Ask her about the pool and the seashells."

I kiss her hand as she grabs the receiver, already happy about the proposed visit and the ocean; I feel I have four, maybe five, minutes before I must say something, solve this.

But there is not much to say. I listen. I commiserate. I am weighed down by Hollywood life, unable to direct a fantasy from this script of convalescence by the sea. I talk with my father, shouting, "How are you?" several times into the phone until my nosy neighbor drops her knitting and comes down her porch steps.

He won't put on his hearing aid. Unreachable in his cancer, he foils us with his deafness. The only thing worse is when he describes the shame, the mess, the lack of dignity, and the pain.

The dog scratches to go out. Feeling trapped, I push open the back door. There will be lilacs this year, I note.

"I love you." Silence, then, "What?" "I love you," I say louder. "I can't hear you. We must have a bad connection." "I love you," I am screaming into the phone. "Oh. Yes. Thank you. Talk to you later. Good-bye."

When David comes back, euphoric from his eight miles of early morning peace, I am waiting, poised in the sunroom. The toys are cleaned up. I want to talk civilly, hug him, ask him about the neighbors he met and his jogging buddy. But I am sitting, hunched, ready, the stone priest with her coffee, her head filled with death.

I breathe slowly through two minutes of his chatter about neighborhood stores on his route, then I am out of control.

"Why can't you get your briefcase out of the living room? And don't park your car in the middle of the walk. You haven't fixed the garage door yet. You never do what you say. Can't you call the carpenter to hang the basketball net for Matthew? He's playing in his room again, and the noise drives me crazy. Why didn't you walk the dog? I can't do breakfast and nag Matthew to walk the dog. I refuse to do the soccer carpool if I'm driving the tennis makeup all the way out to Aspen Hill. Why can't we find a program nearby?"

And on and on. Medusa of the morning coffee. As he does every Saturday, he asks me what's wrong. "Nothing," I hiss as I wind my way upstairs and out of sight.

"Let Go." "Let go," I order my children from the waiting room at Union Station, the point of departure for my frequent trips to New York, the land of infinite medical opinions and two of the best cancer wards in the east. "Don't fight," I tell them, thinking how, with surprising childish fear I want to demand my father beat his advancing cancer, and survive this upcoming operation.

I drag my brown suitcase down the narrow train aisles, searching for a place beyond smoke and newspapers.

I find a seat behind an overweight lady unwrapping what smells like tuna fish with pickles. Unlikely to be found, I sit by the window, my suitcase blockading the other seat. Dug in, I hear the conductor shout "Let's go."

I left my children eight stops back in Washington, waving good-bye their hands filled with Baby Ruths, the red and white wrappers flapping like tiny flags. You wouldn't think that separated by two fathers, one decade, and over a hundred pounds, they could find such meaning in halves of a candy bar, each wanting more.

The bean pole and the midget; more like a circus team than brother and sister. His hair combed to a teenage perfection, but his brown corduroy pants split along the seams, and his "tennis players have fuzzy balls" T-shirt proclaiming insouciance. Her roly-poly face fat with a chocolate smile, barrettes dangling below her ears, laces untied. She's wearing her black sheep jacket, holding his hand. He's looking straight ahead at me as I disappear down the track.

Three candy bars apiece they look curiously placated despite the fact that I told them never to take candy from strangers.

To survive, I disengage. I've become Shadow Mom, a voice of directives broadcasting by rote—did you take your vitamins, do you have your key, return your library books, leave the name of your friend, then be gone.

My mother's frequent phone calls, a mix of fear and nervousness, my father's slow gait, sad eyes, and swift cancer-changes, leave me hollow. Caring for two old people lost in the horrors of a cancer maze of conflicting medical opinions, but certain death, supplants the time for children, gobbling up delight in soccer goals, and construction paper treehouses.

I feed, and clothe, keep track of appointments, remind when possible, read an occasional story, or watch a television show together. Beyond that, I can't be bothered. I am a stranger toting boxes.

I have folded enough things inside for two weeks—silk dresses to talk to doctors in, wool pants for sleeping in intensive care waiting rooms, jeans for cooking, boots against a New York blizzard, and my black suit for funerals, packed last at 3 A.M. when I gave up from exhaustion and my husband's demands for turning out the lights.

Who knows how long these things last? Pack well for there's a sorrow beyond words. I could forget my sleeping socks, and stay awake hours thinking of cold stars.

A shy five with long hair and a crooked grin, I often felt alone, younger than the others and quieter too I sat on the pink stucco porch playing jacks for hours.

Like magic you produced the red bike. Balancing me along the bungalow courtyards, running behind me, you let go so lightly that I biked past three houses till I realized you were gone. "Then, frightened, I looked back and toppled on the pavement, scratching the new chrome and my dirty knees. You held me, and said to keep trying. I made you promise to tell me when you let go.

That summer you taught me my first freedom. Letting that bike go up alleys and down the courtyard, getting enough speed to cross the small sandy patch near the boardwalk, and back down past the pastel bungalows fronting the street, I learned invincibility. After the morning rain, I pedaled fast to the puddle in front of the Schwartz's, picked up my heels, and skimmed the bike through the water without a splash. It felt like floating.

You made your choice. When they told you they stopped the operation because your heart was too weak, you told them to go ahead. "I'd rather die on the table, than die of cancer. Reschedule it."

From the picture windows in the IC waiting lounge, I watch the boats in the East River take leave of the harbor, and the helicopters take off, carrying the important quickly to their next destination. Because of the rain, the darkness slides on. No colors in the sunset but gray.

I hear the rattling of gurneys pushed in and out of the elevators.

"Let the elevator go. I'll take the next one," says an orderly striking up a conversation with a smiling candy striper.

My sister Shelley's with you saying good-bye. My mother waits in the hall by the medication computer. The lady whose husband's kidneys failed after the anesthesia paces up and down, worrying about overcoats brought past the intensive care doors. "They bring germs, you know," she says to no one in particular. "They should put a stop to it."

She will save him by warding off the disease of winter coats.

Businesslike, Shelley hustles my mother in, then walks me down the hall. What will she tell him after 47 years? Three minutes later she's out of the room.

Shelley pushes me past the nurses who order us to leave. "Hours over. We need to prep for tomorrow." "Let it go this time," Shelley says. "We'll be gone soon. I promise."

I walk towards you. My father. Propped up in your hospital bed, anchored by tubes, you look part fragile patriarch, and already part memory. The plastic tubes of the Swan-Ganz connect the vein in your arm to your heart, then drape around your neck and head. The steady flow of red blood pulses a high-tech crown. Your nose is purple from the tubes. Silently, the monitors flash pulse rates, breathing, pressure. Tubes collect urine; the IV stands guard like a Saturday Night scepter.

Bed pans clatter in the background. The old woman with high blood pressure in the next bed moans and wheezes on and on. The drunk in the front cubicle, lost in his delirium, curses the nurses, attempting to cut loose his restraints.

What do I bring out first? I reassure you, tell you we will be here all morning, sending you good energy. I let you know I am proud of your strength, and admiring of your courage.

"The children are fine. David's fine. Writing's tricky, but things will work out," I say, trying to convince both of us. I tell you I will be okay even if I can't explain.

Quietly, I say, "I love you." For the first time you reply, "I love you too." I am crying, but trying not to. The nurse, distracted by our conversation, breaks a connection in your tubes. Behind you your blood spills down the white sheet. You do not notice. I try not to be afraid.

"What will be will be," you say. "I have a lot to live for."

As we exchange long looks, three nurses corral me from your room, telling me our time was up. But I feared they meant yours; and it seemed we were just beginning.

Waiting. I keep reading, looking up only to focus on the bowl of fresh oranges, the vat of hospital coffee, and on the woman whose husband, only slightly surviving triple by-pass surgery, as she stares blankly at the East River.

A tense silence covers all of us; no one talks in the morning while relatives hang between surgical procedures. Shelley dreamt of Dad's drowning, needing to be pulled up from the gray depths of a Rockaway winter ocean.

But it should be over by now. We phone the operation information line every fifteen minutes only to be told "He's not out of surgery yet."

No word about survival, just the aroma of half-eaten oranges, stale hospital coffee, and the incessant padding of the nurses down the corridors.

Two more hours pass, punctuated by our phone calls. I've read the same chapter three times, and I still can't put the characters to places, recall events in sequence.

"Let's not worry," I mutter, ducking into the ladies room to cry alongside a wall beseeching "Call Joyce for a good time."

"Take your lenses out. Your eyes are red," my mother orders, needing not to understand. We trek across the courtyard to huddle in the surgeon's office.

Before he ducks in the back door, I catch his eyes, dark hollows in an ashen face. I bite my lip and motion bad news to my sister.

We file in slowly, and I think, "If he never tells us, will it never happen."

"He survived," says the surgeon. Laughing with relief, and thankfulness, we push away the rest. "You did it, Dad" we think, so proud of you, grateful you can be a stubborn old man with a strong will.

The surgeon cuts through our jubilation with precision, the steel-bladed accuracy of the prognosis is not good. "The cancer too far along, the heart so weak. The next few days will be as difficult as the surgery. Expect him not to respond, not to be conscious, maybe not to survive."

When my mother pushes her way through the recovery room nurses to see my dad, to touch his hand, she comes back quickly, tearful, gagging, shaking her head, overwhelmed by tubes, machinery, and the cold paleness of stainless steel life support machinery.

But even with an all-consuming cancer, small triumphs come. And so we insist on celebration. We whisk my mother away to a feast of Chinese food—hot and sour soup, egg rolls, shrimp, chicken with cashew nuts, beef broccoli, and good fortune cookies.

When I take my mother home to Long Island on the train, we smile at strangers.

Late that night, Shelley says, when she went to see my dad, he was up, briefly joking with the IC nurses, thanking them, shaking hands, jubilant to be alive.

You skillful but person-dumb surgeon, you know not the staunch stock I come from, or how strong a wish can be.

Toward Spring. With each visit, Dad, you shrink before my eyes. Whittled by the cancer, you've become almost a miniature of the father I remember. Weaker and weaker, each time, when you see me, you struggle a bit more to hug, and your voice cracks with weariness, but your eyes smile brightly.

You complain about the cold. I bring you bright Izod sweaters—yellow, green, burgundy, and three shades of blue—in smaller and smaller sizes. You gripe about the frequent bathroom urges, speak bitterly of the cancer, and the doctors who urged useless treatments, notable only for their pain, and indignity.

You demand to know when you will be better. I do not know how to tell you, or when you will really understand there is no better, only the terrifying specter of much worse.

Passover. There is always the hope that the angel of death will pass over my house this year. Tonight, we are only three, my son visiting in New York, my sisters scattered, my parents sequestered in Florida. The smallness of our group aggravates David. But I am relieved.

Too tired to contact friends, I feel too morose for invitations.

Only my small daughter, prepped with two weeks of nursery school cardboard cutouts of seder plates and matzoh, looks forward to the service. And the dog who waits for scraps.

We cook turkey out of habit. Mix dates with apples and sugar for sweetness, and put out the cup for Elijah, a sly wiseman full of riddles for answers.

I take cover behind the two dozen pink tulips, coming out only to dazzle my daughter with promises. Like you taught me, Dad, I ceremoniously break the Afikomen, speak of treasure for those who find it, then walk pink panther-like across the living room to almost hide the matzoh behind a crocheted cushion.

When Elijah comes, just as you did, Dad, I open the door, and while Alissa peers at the wine in his cup, shake the table to signal Elijah's drinking. He is here. Amazed, she giggles and stamps her feet with delight.

Such tricks were yours, Dad.

Up through Elijah, I tolerated your absence. After that, I break the matzoh into pieces, nervously stuffing bits into my mouth, the crumbs cascading down my blouse. My daughter protests it's not time to eat yet. My husband, in his all too familiar gesture of toleration, continues on.

But with Elijah all the ghosts of my childhood rush in. Their voices sing three-part harmonies of "Dayenu," and "Chad Gadya." A ragtime "Shehecheyanu" tumbles in my livingroom.

Aunt Clara's four room apartment bursts with relatives. They start on cardtables in the foyer, and spill into the living room on couches pushed up close to tables lined with benches and kitchen chairs. Three cousins fill each side chair.

Dark haired ladies with smiling eyes bring steaming bowls of matzoh ball soup, plates of gefilte fish. I could eat that as it had no head and looked like a potato. I wondered how they swam with no eyes. Platters of brisket, and turkey lined with gravy appear magically from the kitchen.

Amazed, I sat and watched. You yelled at me, half urging, half commanding me to play with these once-a-year cousins in a room piled high with living-room coats and purses the size of a valise.

Shy, I disappointed you, wanting to watch the adults. And the singing.

You led with your brother Aaron; both reclined on bedroom pillows, the harmonies are tight and joyful. You sang the songs you sang as a boy with your parents in a Manhattan tenement that I dreamed smelled of roast chicken and macaroons.

The harmonies with all your sisters and brothers filled the tiny apartment. Aaron with his bass like gravel. Jennie, Gussie, and Clara sang a smooth contralto. Harry adding a melody. You, a smooth tenor rounding out the rhythms.

All the singers are dead now. Except you and Clara, and she is blind.

My dining room is small and empty. There are no songs and only a ten-minute seder punctuated by my matzoh cracking.

Why is this night different from all other nights? Because I don't want to sit in your place at this seder, reclining on cushions, leading.

I fear your disintegration into memory. That moment when I will have two bars of melody to sustain me on a windy night when I am walking home alone to a house full of grown children.

I try to tell my husband. I am lost wandering, cut loose this whole year. Friends whisper, "Remember to breathe." I squint at people through long tunnels. Grief hangs in the air like mist.

With no Moses to guide me I seek my own golden calf in the shape of old fantasies. To sleep, I count long-haired hippies, bare-chested, muscular and lean, singing old rock tunes. The sun dances off a row of guitars. One by one these young men jump to the rock rhythms of Joplin, Hendrix, Morrison.

All dead now.

So I flirt with Ben, too young and much too pretty. We speak safe words like "modem," "disk drive," "surge protector," while I almost tell him yes, I will meet him at the beach where he sings and plays saxophone in a rock band. Yes, it would feel good to dance in a room filled with smoke and laughter, make love with the cool sand on my back.

But I am still waiting.

The day Kevin booked a flight to Portland to bring his mother, terminal with cancer, east, he screwed his lab assistant on the office couch, danced with her till midnight, then came home and confessed to his wife. The next morning he carried his mother on board the Eastern jet, laid her across three seats, too weak to sit, and brought her home to die as she wished, in a room next to her only grandchild.

The year pancreatic cancer ate Debra's father, she left her childhood sweetheart and husband of 7 years, moved across town to cry at night in a faux-medieval townhouse.

There is solace nowhere; just waiting. Wayne kept bowling. Each night when the cancer ward closed down for visitors, he kissed his mother's balding head, held her hands bony with intravenous tubes, then escaped the 18 miles through the city's darkened tunnels to a Brooklyn bowling alley ringed with '64 Chevys and dayglow vans.

Only hurling those dark black balls like cannon down the slick alley, then waiting the four seconds for the heavy crack and thud of pins could temporarily knock the sound of cancer from his ears.

Frame after frame he bowled. The last one to leave, the crush of pins echoed down the cavernous room. He kept throwing balls until the manager in the red polyester jersey and Yankees cap turned off the lights, one by one.

Alone is how watching death feels. And all my losses double back upon me, echoing in my head. I feel them all now from the time my third grade best friends, twins, moved away to the high school lover lost to a different college, to the marriage that unraveled under the pressures of diapers, adulthood, and final exams, the book stillborn, the baby dead.

I move like one caught in a net. Old losses and fantasies stick to my sides like webbing, especially the fantasy about a perfect father-daughter relationship. There will be no resolution.

Whatever was, is.

Escape and Acceptance. As I crest the Allegheny Mountains, hazy in the morning light, sweeping through hillsides purple with rhododendron, I listen for your melodies, Dad, my songs of childhood.

When I phone, for the first time, I hear the dry thinness in your voice. Between thanking me for the VCR, and complaining about your legs, you evaporate between pauses. For both of us, the conversation is like coming up for air.

"I cannot walk. My legs swell like piano legs. I pant, I struggle, I need to sit."

I offer up wheelchairs.

You tell me of making peace, but your words rise in a cry like a Yiddish lullaby, melancholic and filled with nearby trouble.

Engulfed, dragged under, we gulp for words. Against the silences, I frantically click change into the phone booth.

What to say when we both know you are fading.

At Burnside Bridge in Sharpsburg, MD, the site of the bloodiest battle of the Civil War, the trees reach over the creek banks, and the ferns are full of butterflies. Nearby at Sunken Lane where the blood from 4,000 casualties ran in rivulets, wildflowers grow now.

I keep walking and taking notes.

Sent here to imagine the fierce incongruity of death on a fine Indian summer morning, I seek to outrun images of dying.

How do you escape asks Shelley, my Brooklyn Heights sister who's facing this with me. I hit the road and keep traveling. "Have you seen a wild turkey lately?" I ask, avoiding all further discussion.

All along Fifteen Mile Creek in Green Ridge, the forest fills with the sound of birds, and the soft rush of water. I see a deer drink at the pond near the apple orchards, and the stand of Hemlock feels cool and feathery.

The ranger and I compare outlooks. He has No Name where the Potomac winds purple in the distance, and West Virginia floats, a series of green hills full of promises.

I have the flat blackness of questions.

I've hit my stride, another 100 miles to go today. I'm moving at high speed past the crests of Backbone and Meadow Mountains where the coal glints in the afternoon sun, and the meadows bloom yellow with blackeyed Susans and daisies.

On the first day of spring I wake in an eccentric Victorian bed in Appalachia in a house full of strangers. My car is covered with snow. The elements here defy all logic.

Intent on warm weather, I have packed only cotton pants and open-toed shoes. Dutifully, I hike the mile of slush to Muddy Creek Falls' 51 feet of cascading white water, thinking only of my cold toes, taking notes for August daytrippers.

Journalism, like dying, has a three month leadtime. First I try to remember, then to understand.

Summer. The ritual of the summer vacation endures even with
the specter of cancer. From my balcony, the Blue Ridge Mountains
are dappled with blues and greens, a mountain aerie for escape.

This day I take Matthew riding. As I drive down the mountain
speckled with laurels, the sweet morning air promises a good day's
journey through the hillsides on horseback. As we saddle up, we
watch Dancer, the owner's stallion, gallop frantically across his
paddock, a picture of power, ribs outlined against a tough suede skin,
snorting in the sun.

What makes him refuse to jump the fence?

As we leave the paddock, the slight echo of horse hooves on the
gravel reassures me, and the trail pops into red rhododendrons.

When the leader raises her hand, our column takes flight. It takes
all my concentration to balance and stay with my horse.

Cantering through the pine forest the boy scouts planted 30 years
ago, I feel almost free again. The coolness seduces, and the ground
crackles as the hooves drive the dried needle covering apart. I lose
almost all my sadness in concentration, ducking branches, balancing,
swinging through the curved path, keeping up.

Those boy scouts, middle-aged like me now, maybe fat and
balding, slinking through a bad marriage, or weaving through a high-
rise in Milwaukee, took root here.

I thank them for their steadfastness. Moving with the
purposefulness of nine-year-olds, dragging shovels in a barren field,
they planted seedlings. Now, only a few low branches touch the backs
of horses. Most arch above the riders, offering cool tunnels suffused
with the scent of pine mountains.

When we stop by the lake to rest the horses, Poor Dog, the
leader's mutt, breaks from us, barking.

It's the doe on the far bank he wants. Frightened the doe flees into
the water, frantically splashing, sending chaotic circles of white water

through the lake, squealing, weighed down by her own fear. But moving slowly. Poor Dog, swiftly, deftly, almost effortless, paddles to the doe's side, bites her neck, and holds on. We watch in silent horror, a cadre of Sunday horsemen struck down from our perfect summer morning.

The doe fights valiantly, powerfully jerking her head in an attempt to loose Poor Dog's grasp. But a crescendo of her squeals shoot backward through the forest. Her blood radiates a muddy red pool in the lake water near the battle site. She flails, jerks her head, kicks.

Her squeals mix with the sound of gulped water, and brief silences as she's dragged under. Next, the burst of breaking water as she cuts free momentarily in a surge of energy and a will to live. Poor Dog hardly looks tired.

My mouth begins to scream. I call the dog, demand his obedience, scream at our guide to chase back Poor Dog. I head my horse into the lake, a lone ranger to the rescue. Brought back by my guide with a remonstrance of the lake's depth, and my steed's flightiness, I curse, and wail. My voice grows raspy screaming, "Let go. Let go. Stop. Let her live." I dismount and throw rocks at Poor Dog, a feeble gesture as his distance saves him from my bad aim. I grab handfuls of pebbles, and tear grass from the lake-side, my fingers scratched and bleeding. The sweat drips down my shirt.

Stuck in our sunlight, paralyzed riders, we are helpless.

Imploring, begging, weeping, I cannot watch, yet I cannot leave her. The woman behind me vomits; Matthew, my teenager, looks dumbfounded. Our country guide, only mildly ruffled, reminds us this is nature, but I keep chaotically heaving pebbles at Poor Dog, half a lake away.

The doe's squeals hit a staccato rhythm that ends in a surge of water. She's gone, and the only sound is Poor Dog paddling toward us. I fantasize trampling him with my horse.

Poor Dog bounces triumphantly from the lake, his breast spotted with the doe's blood. We ride slowly back to the barn; the Virginia sun burns my back.

My husband asks how the ride was. I cannot answer.

That night from my balcony, coffee cup in hand, I painstakingly count the stars as they pop, and glow against the soft purple sky. Matthew comes along beside me, touching my arm.

"It's grandpa isn't it?"

Caught in your cancer, held steadfastly in its mongrel teeth, my father, I am a rider powerless to save you. With fall I know the best will be long gone, the cancer bitten deep into your body, a beast that won't let go.

And we the helpless voyeurs.

Some moments of your pure fight amaze me. Keeping your head above the den couch, carefully dressed in street clothes each morning, you watch television. Swaddled amid baseball scores and front page news, you look like Sunday morning.

But the blankets wrapped about you belie your bony body. You still laugh at my daughter offering you jelly beans with a fat, four-year-old fist.

You spend evenings in the bathroom spewing blood. Even you refuse to know how sick you are.

The Next Fall: Marriage, the Mundane and Mourning. The brightly colored pages of department store catalogues transfix me. Wrap me in a grey cashmere evening coat, a tawny Burberry's rain coat, an angled Kasper suit with fuchsia jacket, or a flowing Adrianna Papell silk dress. I search for new meaning with Harve Bernard, Chanel, Liz Claiborne, and Perry Ellis.

I melt into incessant shopping in D.C.'s flashy stores—Saks,

Neiman-Marcus, Bloomingdale's—trying to muffle the hurt, cover over the images of thin dying, with yards and yards of yuppie finery.

I'm on a quest. Armed with car keys, and plastic credit, each Saturday forms a new test of wits. In this medley of mall noises, let cancer not exist, and loss be merely a temporary mistake, a wayward item to be credited to a future account.

Fill me up with things. I move dazed by all the possibilities, nerves quietly calmed by the almost surreal images—trees blooming with yellow, pink, and blue Papagallo shoes, triplet mannequins defiant in identical black chemises, belted tautly with rows and rows of glistening gold belts, and glass walls draped with handknit tops, blazing with geometric flashes of color.

In this perverse American dream, let things be the annihilator of insidious pain, and slow death. Earth tone linen beiges, soft, fine Scottish wools, and delicate Chinese hand-painted silks, cascade out the top of my shopping bags. Swaddled, sated, bundled, bulging with middle-class goodies, I drive home.

And then we fight. In a world where I am lost in melancholy and silence you, my husband, leap at me with jealous jettes; charge account bills become the tight connection to our hearts.

I want it, I say. I mean you. I'll pay, I swear, and silently count the requisite stories I must sell. Still, your curses land atop my shopping bags with tax accountant accuracy. You want me to save my money for your partnership, a future bigger house. You fail to understand long-term holds little meaning, and abstractions no delight.

We refuse to speak.

Last Holidays. Determined to follow tradition, you painstakingly go to temple for Rosh Hashanah. I meet you there for your alia. Less than 100 pounds, it takes you almost half an hour to walk a small path to the door. You had no sons. Before you go to the bimah, I

whisper, amid the centuries-old melodies of Jews, "I promise to say
Kaddish for you." Distracted by 1000 spectators, and constant page-
turning, we speak the first conversation about your death.

You smile an ancient blessing, and while the congregation turns
to follow the torah to the back of the temple, Harry, your friend for
40 years, gently leads you to the front. This day that life is inscribed, I
look for miracles.

Shelley and I pray for your health, Mom cries, and I grab the
evening shuttle home to children and a stack of student term papers,
muttering to myself like a lost bag lady.

Thanksgiving, you prop yourself up valiantly, for us and for your
visiting friends, your presence a triumph, the cancer momentarily
pushed down, you manage the entire meal, until dessert. Then fall
asleep, sitting upright at the table, skinnier than the turkey bone.
Eaten through.

I am afraid. The specter of more pain for you scares me; shocked
by your thinness, I can no longer pretend you will not suffer or die.

Scraping the interminable dinner plates, loading the dishwasher, I
lose layers of defenses at the thought of your coming death. Cut raw,
terrified at being without your chuckle, I must come clean.

It's undeniable now, even to me. The game is up. You're dying.

I am Alice, instantly shrinking from career woman to little girl
lost in a strange and disturbing landscape. Just like the time I got left
on the boardwalk in the sudden rain, I panic, and look frantically for
you to save me from the crowds.

I scrape plates faster, a manic mad housekeeper. Hanging in an
uncertain marriage, following a difficult career, two children to raise, I
need to drink in your genuine hello from time to time. Whose smile
will anchor me? Even in my dreams, who will protect me from the
red Queen's fury?

I sit a long time at the kitchen table, clutching my teacup.

All week, I work, mind children, confer with doctors, social workers, listen to my dying father, cat-nervous mother, and muffle my own pain in quick turn around assignments, and successive committee meetings.

I cannot accompany my husband to dinner parties, or PTA meetings. I can no longer speak little chit-chat, or smile at gossip. My witty conversation self-aborts at inception, squeezed out by loss.

"Bob and Lisa don't understand why you didn't come to his birthday party. I had to cover for you," intones my husband.

"Tell them," I say flatly, "that it is hard to eat ice cream, and sing after just arriving home from seeing one's father dirty with cancer, or watch one's mother weep with pain."

"We are losing the Rosens as friends."

And we did. Whenever they see me buying toothpaste at the drugstore, picking up the kids at carpool, or walking in the park, they smile coldly.

I do too at their pure innocence of life that hasn't yet given them tumors, bleeding, and inevitable loss.

Some friends understand why I am absent, shut up from parties this year, too sad to talk of bargain Volvos, best vacations, or propose solutions for the homeless.

On my biweekly jaunts to New York, I cry in airport waiting areas surrounded by student papers. In New York, no one even notices. In Washington, travelers stare almost kindly.

Hollowed out by my visits where I juggle disbelief, horror, and hope in my parents' living room amid the light lunches, trying not to see my father fade away, or notice the blood stained clothing, I return home, feeling decades older, and etched in stone.

"I am empty," I tell you, my husband, I'm ordering Chinese food, my old ally in sadness. When I ask if you want anything, you turn slowly from the kitchen counter, taunting like a street thug.

"How could you buy Chinese food? Inconsiderate. How could you be away all day, leaving the kids? How come you never pay any attention to me?" And on and on.

But this time, instead of leaving the room, dignity only partially unhitched, I collapse on the kitchen floor, and wail.

Blackness and tears and unending loss. My four-year-old, horrified, puts her arms around me. I am crying, uncontrollably, wiping my nose on my sleeve, weeping. "I ordered an egg roll and soup. What do you want from me?"

Hours of marriage counseling later, I learn my turning inward, weariness, and your own fears and tiredness, provoked your rage. But now that I've felt the limits of your empathy, witnessed your tiny rageful child screaming at me when I must be tending to another, I wonder how long it will take before I can forgive you, and if I can shrink the boundaries of my own neediness.

Whoever said adversity makes couples grow closer was never married, never dealt with carpools in the midst of malignant tumors, billable law office hours when homework assignments need reading, or pondered committee meetings when medical treatments conflict, deadlines when children want bedtime stories and teenagers driving lessons, or faced hopeless death, weakness, and emptiness when the dog needs walking, the dinner watching, and the garden weeding.

Impossible, I tell everyone, then clam up, the stone priestess to high perfection.

The Hospice. At the hospice, settled in a corner room that catches the steel glint of the sun off the Bronx rooftops, only your perpetually dark skin, and your smiling eyes remind me of you, and the beach summers of my childhood.

Before the rest, when the morning felt soft and feathery, we'd wake up, buy rolls still warm at the baker's, then walk the long block to the water. You'd tote the blanket, and cooler filled with juice, and I, my pail, shovel, and strainer.

I'd race you up the boardwalk and down the stairs to the beach, always just winning. The tiny pebbles in the sand catch the sun, turning this morning beach to bright crystal pop jewelry.

We're the first here as always. Just us. Holding hands in blue-gray Rockaway ocean, flat with the morning, we practice floating. Then, you'd encourage my hesitant swimming by moving backwards slowly, forcing me to cut through the growing surf, and breathe my way alone longer. Only the slight tide and the baby gulls hopping and shouting in the dark sand, break the perfect morning stillness.

During the day, the hospice makes no noise. In the cab, I imagined people gnarled through by cancer, shouting, moaning, a Hieronymus Bosch nightmare. Toting Miller, your favorite beer, rainbow drawings from my daughter, and bringing Matthew, I walk the long hall to your room. But the stillness of this last beach head, and the bright windows surprise me. Only the muffled rumble of the cars on the highway just beyond break the linoleum quiet. Resting on gurneys pushed into the corridor, these last fighters float calmly, held aloft by powerful medications.

I come to hold your hand. Today, it's almost only your eyes I recognize as you recede before me. Your skin taut about your cheek bones, your arms bruised from incessant scratching, itching a side effect of the useless medication. Yet you kick the cancer down, defying death predictions for an audience of stupefied doctors.

So thin, the doctors won't even let you shuffle slowly to the bathroom, you balance dignity and defiance, lamenting why 73 years should come to this.

I tell you I love you.

Matthew and I gather round your bed, each taking turns, mixing small talk with last statements. Matt tells you how the Knicks did; I pop open the beer.

"Remember me," you say crying.

With the cancer bitten through to bone, you complain the sharp pain comes like waves on top of a never-ending discomfort, necessitating constant calls for the orderly. One of them talks respectfully, and carries you to the bathroom; the other steals your watch.

You want to die, but fear and longing hold you here. At night, you sleep fitfully, half-calling, half-crying "mama mama mama" down the corridors of a long-away Manhattan tenement. Such melodies, I'm told, regularly mix with the footsteps of the nurses in the night hallways.

With old-fashioned stubbornness, you refuse to use the bed pan, wanting the dignity of walking to the bathroom. But like a fragile new-born bird, your legs collapse under you. Face down on the floor, weeping, several times a night the orderlies carry you to your bed.

So weak you cannot feed yourself, or hold a telephone, or speak more than three words in one breath, but at night you climb over the steel bed railings, hopping, falling on the floor.

Enough, says the logical doctor, thinking about hips and law suits. He prescribes, for your safety, he says, and the efficient use of his staff, a restraining jacket. Straitjacketed, your hands cuffed to the railings, tiny, shriveled, not eating,—I beg them to do something else—you are still Dad of the stubborn old man, not giving an inch to cold bureaucracy.

Each night, wanting to leave, requesting your hat and coat, slyly, swiftly, magically, you undo your restraining jacket, Houdini style, climb the rails, and fall on the floor. No one knows how you jump this barrier, momentarily beating the cancer down.

Shelley explains escape is not that way. Begging them to find a way to untie you, we reassure you we will all be all right. "Stay connected," you command. We plan your funeral together.

Naomi, the cantor whose melodies float through this Catholic hospice, comforting the Jewish patients, will sing the Elmoly Rachamim, the Jewish song of dying. Your nephew will speak, and all your three daughters.

"I can be alone," I whisper to you, propelled on my own, with children in tow. "We all can," we say.

"Free yourself from pain, and indignity," we repeat, blessing your leave taking. "Let go, and rest."

A large head with weeping eyes, wrapped in white linen like a shroud, you think it over.

The next day, with your wife of 47 years in the room, you wait for your favorite nephew's afternoon phone call. With Mom, connected, talking to him, you open your eyes, and fly away.

After. The day you died New York City took five inches of snow. I drove the turnpike by myself, children and all, periodically knocking the ice off the headlights, choosing the rhythms of long-distance driving to transport me to this new time without you.

The day we buried you the wind whistled down the long rows of tombstones, and the graveyard mud turned to ice. Matthew and your other grandsons carried your casket to that gaping hole; but I whispered to them not to worry, for you weren't really there. "Look up; Grandpa will help us from the other side."

The day after, four more inches of snow quieted the city. Leaving my shiva box, and a room full of persistent relatives, I kept walking those icy streets, a lone figure, searching for solace in some take-out won-ton soup.

Trudging back, cheeks red with the cold, hands numb, I stopped at the light for the one cab pushing through the snow. With my head bent in the take-out boxes to catch the steam off the soup, as the crossing green came, I thought I caught a strain of a ragtime She-hec-heyanu. I smiled and walked the long way home.

HOW DO YOU LIKE
 YOUR BLUEEYED BOY,
MISTER DEATH

—e.e. cummings

DEA ADRIA MALLIN

EVERYONE ELSE REMEMBERS THE day JFK died; I remember the day my father died.

In my family, I am a kind of Cassandra. The truth makes its way to me, flows to me like water seeking the path of least resistance. I have never been afraid of the truth . . . even when I was very small and my mother would lift my brother and me to the window seat to watch in the night for my father's homecoming. It was very dark and the winter cold would seep through the windowpane and make me shiver in my Dr. Dentons. There were nights my father did not come home until early morning, and although my mother never said a word, never gave shape to her fears, never explained anything, long after we were out of Dr. Dentons and had lives of our own to occupy every waking moment, in my dreams I knew that one day Daddy really wouldn't come home.

Only I had to remain mute. There was no place in my family—or perhaps anywhere in those post-war days of three square meals, Saturday matinees, and renewed faith—for anything but the pursuit of happiness.

Instead, I was ever alert to the disaster awaiting a family with a father who gambled. Whether to answer an internal cry or the externals of a wife and three children, he gambled. As Cassandra, I would distract my mother and sister when they would lean hungrily over the Hermes handbag counter. "Daddy doesn't make that kind of money," I whispered to the countertops.

When he was only fourteen years old, my father had been touted by the newspapers as the youngest freshman ever admitted to the ivy halls of his distinguished university. He had held his brilliant head up among older and sturdier freshmen in their beanies by playing cards like a wizard until the weary dawn, then going straight to classes and getting A's. By the time he was my father, he was playing bridge with Charles Goren and placing his bets on horses from fancy clubhouses. But his income as a lawyer was not adequate to the gambler he was becoming. Too soon, three teenage children would displace him into middle age ("old age," if my brother was correct) when he would face bills for three college tuitions.

I adored my father. I have his shell-shaped ears, his even teeth, his long legs, and, like my father, I never needed anything fancy to make me feel alive. Like me, he mused on creation and destruction, everything and nothing, and so felt compelled to tease the syllables of language into poems. I think I had the only father in the neighborhood who, without getting hit by a car, could walk all the way home from the 6 o'clock train reading *The New York Times* without looking up. He was the only father coming home in his business suit on a sweltering evening before air conditioners who would turn the jump rope for us so that all the girls could jump double dutch. And surely he was the only father on the block

bellowing out Rudyard Kipling verses from the shower in un-
abashed tunelessness.

*****

I suppose we were nearly grown, the three of us, by that summer,
and perhaps that made it easier for him to choose to exit the planet.

It was late August—lazy and hot and a time to wrap up before
autumn. My father was scheduled to arrive at the Philadelphia
Airport from a meeting with Atlanta clients at 8 P.M. I had returned
that afternoon from my summer camp job as waterfront counselor.
My brother, just back from hitchhiking across the United States in
preparation for writing The Great American Novel, was flinging his
filthy stuff into the laundry room. My sister was due home in a few
days from study in Mexico to share our room again.

At 11:30 P.M., after a date with my summer boyfriend, I bounced
in the front door where my mother met me, an oddly familiar
distraught look consuming her pretty face. Daddy had not come
home. Yes, he had been a passenger aboard the plane, and no, there'd
been no mishaps nor delays.

Then why wasn't he home yet?

My mother picked up the phone to call her closest friend,
Lillian—"Aunt" Lillian to us—her fear visibly mounting. Pragmatic
and level-headed Lillian counseled my mother to drive to the airport
to seek more information. My mother turned to my brother, and they
made the 45-minute drive together, leaving me behind. They had
their mutual company and their joint mission as a defense to keep the
mind in check. I remained stationary, the appointed guardian of the
telephone, but my mind drove the road of every imaginable disaster.
Daddy had fallen. Daddy'd had a heart attack. Daddy had careened
off the road. Daddy had been abducted at gunpoint in some bizarre
case of mistaken identity.

My mother and brother returned from the airport. Nothing.

It was late and too gruesome to contemplate a round of hospital calls since there was still the chance that towards dawn we would each hear from our separate rooms Daddy's footsteps bounding up the stairs and some rational explanation in the morning. Exhausted, we fell asleep, and while we slept, the rational world simply slipped away.

Dawn brought only the jarring sound of the telephone with Aunt Lillian on the other end of the wires. My mother stood there like a wraith, her voice small and mechanical, the color draining from her face. My brother and I, having sprung from our beds to race for the phone, now clutched the doorway woodwork as if it could hold us up against hopelessness.

My mother turned again to my brother. Lillian would pick them up and the three of them would drive to the Airport Motel where my father was. I would follow twenty minutes later in the family car. There was no way to contemplate the meaning of this two-step. I dressed without knowing the clothes had touched my body. At last there was something for me to do, a clear directive, a move towards closure. Was I to brush my teeth as well as dress? I had twenty minutes. I brushed my teeth for all twenty.

As I got into the family car, I wondered what you call a family car if the father is dead.

Behind the wheel, I flicked on the radio to dispel the spectral and regain the ordinary. The DJ announced a song from *The Sound of Music*. If I can sing, I thought, I'll be okay, I'll be steady. I opened my mouth so that Julie Andrews and I could have one voice. "Climb every mountain, ford every stream," her liquid power filled the car and rushed by my ears on its way out the window. "Follow every rainbow till you find your dream."

If he's dead, I said to myself, my mouth contrarily forming each syllable of the radio song, if he's dead, I'll find that dream and I won't let go. Why would he let go? Will somebody tell me why people let go? "A wonderful thing is the end of a string and will somebody tell me why people let go?" e.e. cummings was Daddy's own poet. Why would Daddy let go?

I remember thinking, "I can't see the road anymore. There are tears all over the road." But I kept on because the song kept on, croaking at the top of my lungs on the Schuylkill Expressway at 6:27 A.M. at 70 mph about finding the dream when I was speeding towards the nightmare, and I knew then that life would always be two things at once—it would be hope and despair, alive and dead, joy in the climb and clinging to the dream right next to the choking sadness and madness of the final appointment in Samarra, my appointment with my father's destiny which was waiting at the Airport Motel. "Your father has been found."

*****

For years, I could not turn my head to the left as I drove past the airport, or I would have to see the Airport Motel. Even after they tore it down to build a bigger better airport, even without turning my head, I would see the door to the motel room. The maid. The police. Aunt Lillian. Not my mother or my brother. Or my father. I never got to say good-bye. Perhaps this is yet another good-bye. . . .

I barely remember the funeral. I don't know where I sat or who came up to me or even recall the casket. But I can remember my Uncle Murray because he looked like a taller and more dashing double of my father. At the cemetery, Uncle Murray's body shook with his sobbing.

There's Daddy, I conjured, *racked with sobs for someone who is being lowered into the ground. But who is that in the casket?* That wasn't Daddy after all. Those were Uncle Murray's shoulders heaving uncontrollably for the loss of his little brother, my father.

What in an entire life could have prepared a young girl to give her own father to a cold and unforgiving earth?

In Jewish tradition, the mourners "sit shiva" after the funeral. Like the Irish wake and the Jamaican Nine Night, this is supposed to be a time of rending garments in communal awareness of our short stay here, followed by a return to life. Our house, then, was open to family, friends, and people who were strangers to me. My father had died suddenly the day before, the tree of life had just uprooted, and I didn't want a single stranger in my house, the house of my father's footsteps and laughter. If they came, they would trample the garden of memory. I needed to tend that garden that was all I would ever have again of the man I loved best in all the world.

The normalcy of people's voices and their relentless coming and going and eating food and talking about food and their sudden silence if I came near impelled me away from the offenders and up to the solace of my room. We Americans are very bad at death. We need to rend garments together a little more, so that we can dance better together afterwards. The conspiracy of silence and the pervasive myth that death can be kept at bay are not good for the mournful ones. So I sat on my bed, mournful and alone.

Into that space came the rabbi from the synagogue. He sat down on my bed with me. Is it written in some commentary that a rabbi can simply enter? No doubt he thought he was comforting me when he told me that although my father was not an observant Jew (in fact, he said that my father was "not a good Jew"—referring to my father's agnostic stance and his occasional attendance at synagogue), I (a "good confirmand") should come to services and not ignore the synagogue. In that moment, I understood why my father did not go to the synagogue.

My father, though he was a gambler and though he took his own life, knew more about lovingkindness than this man of authority could ever hope to extend to the sufferer. So I answered the rabbi, to whom I previously had never said a disagreeable word. "My father was a very religious man; he had deep regard for all living things."

Yes, but. . . . The rabbi seemed to go on and on, bringing his pompousness so easily affected from the pulpit into the intimacy of my retreat.

When he left, I closed the door.

Soon, a gentle knock announced that Aunt Lillian was there. Always a devotee of this rabbi, she did not defend him when I cried, relating the story. Instead, she too began to cry, and I recognized that her tears were not merely for me or for my father; those tears were watering a long-ago pair of graves. She had been just thirteen, in a country in the throes of the Great Depression, when she was orphaned by her parents' double suicide.

"Did you forgive them?" I asked quietly.

"Yes," she said. "They couldn't help themselves."

At that moment, she ceased to be "Aunt" Lillian and became Lillian, my friend.

I had forgiven my father immediately. I am a born forgiver. With a sixth sense for others' pain, I knew that my father's hurt must have been so intense that there was no light, no windows to let in the light.

That night, I slipped into my brother's room. "Do you blame Daddy?" I asked.

He looked thoughtful and then said flatly, "No."

"Good," I answered. "Neither do I."

My father had taught me well about cosmic ironies—laughter and tears and what twins they really are, separated by an invisible thread spun by a fragile silkworm. And he had taught me about compassion and forgiveness.

Yet I cannot say that in the years since his death I have seen much of that in response to suicide. Instead, there are labels and scorn. And fear. About the most the media has done is to give talk show time to survivors' rage, as if there were only one formulaic response to suicide. Indeed, I have met the ones who nurse their rage to keep it warm.

But I think they have missed the message of the suicide and the chance to learn about loving.

"*The rock,*" my mother always called my father. It was too large a myth for him to carry. No one is a rock. My father was just a man, clothed in his own particular humanity. The brilliant son and lawyer; the husband swinging my mother off her feet when he came home from the office and whirling her around and around, her 1950s skirts everywhere at once; the father who recounted fairy tales deep into the night to his spellbound children. This was my father at his best. And then there was the rest.

*****

This year I turned the age my father was when he died. I still do the *New York Times* Sunday crossword puzzles in ink, just as my father used to do, and the pleasure I take as my pen makes its finishing strokes is like no other because it resurrects his concentration and erudition, and the way he sat in his green "daddy chair" finishing off an entire box of good chocolates and the puzzle in sweet synchronicity. I try to do something else I remember him doing. I listen very carefully when others speak because he always took the time to bend toward me and listen to me. His answers revealed how delicately he had heard my lines—and read between them. Small wonder that I now teach a course in interpersonal communication. I think that the phoenix that rises from the ashes is feathered in love, and that love takes wing and alights on those in need. . . .

My father's grave and my husband's grave are now side by side— the two people who gave me the deepest love and the most joyful laughter of my live.

One thing I know about this journey we all make—and it is not easy to distill experience and draw wisdom from it when there is enduring pain—is that it is possible to have lost twice—and still have been twice blessed.

SUMMER EVENING

ELAINE ERICKSON

In loving memory of
Iver Erickson, 1903–1991

I'LL NEVER FORGET THAT early Sunday morning in
August. The sky was a drooping gray canvas over Baltimore City.
The birds had just begun to sing a counterpoint of notes as if to break
through the sky. Suddenly the telephone's rude ring cut into my
reverie. It was my brother Jim, and I knew instantly that something
was wrong. Jim rarely called me. Then I heard those dreaded words:
"Our Dad died last night."

My first reaction was disbelief. How could Iver be gone (I called
my father by his first name in his later years, for we were such close
friends), Iver, who had always been so strong, who comforted me
even when Alzheimer's Disease raged through his body and mind like
a merciless midwestern storm?

My father had started a dairy in Des Moines, Iowa. In 1930 it
was a small business with only three workers and one milk route.

Gradually, he built it up to a huge milk processing plant serving all of Iowa. As a child, I walked carefully through the dairy, where water slid in rivers over the tile floors. I was fascinated by the roar of machinery, milk gushing like gossip. There were rainbows of tulips surrounding the plant in spring, and people came from miles around to take pictures. I was in awe of Iver for building something so big—I was so proud of my Dad.

Now, in Baltimore on that Sunday morning, I felt like a mechanical doll as I got dressed, made plane reservations to Des Moines for Iver's funeral. There was a tight fist in my chest. I must cancel my turn to play the piano for the morning service at church today, I thought. But Iver seemed to be talking to me, comforting me, telling me not to grieve for him, to go ahead and do what I had planned. So I played the piano at church, then took the long rough flight to Des Moines. The fist in me grew tighter, harder. I was still a mechanical doll in a dream.

On the night when Iver's body was to be viewed at the funeral home, I arrived early. I was alone in the room with my father, who seemed to rest peacefully in his casket. His face, though, was strangely pale and waxen. The electronic organ pumped "Sweet Hour of Prayer" through the speakers. Gradually the people began to come, hundreds of them over a four-hour period—dairy employees, people from church, neighbors—all to pay tribute to my Dad. They stood in little groups and chatted—a cacophony of words and laughter—while Iver lay lifeless, silent in his casket.

The large church was packed for the funeral. Again, I was a mechanical doll walking with my family down the aisle. At the end of the service the whole congregation sang the hymn, "Jesus Is Coming Again," a tune that Mother and I had sung with Iver many times in his nursing-home room.

Now, there was nothing to do but go home. But where was

home? My mother lived in a retirement home cottage. My plane for Baltimore didn't leave until the next day. The only place that was home in Iowa was the large white house on John Patterson Road where I grew up. It stood fully furnished but empty of people. It was waiting for me.

Inside, the rooms were filled with dramas. The reflections in the windows were eyes from the past. Memories stepped out of every photograph. My piano was still where it always had been, the one where I played Mozart, Brahms, my own compositions. Iver grew to love my original pieces in his later years. I sank down into my father's favorite chair and suddenly flood gates let loose the tears. The fist is my chest slowly unclenched. I must have cried for hours. . . .

> "Daddy, the lie I told. . . ."
> You sit on the edge of my bed,
> telling me God forgives
> as far as the east is from the west . . .
> Our walks at dusk, the sun's
> burning face peering through the weeds . . .
> At the top of the hill I turn and wave to you
> and you wave back, your silver hair a crown. . . .

My mind drifted. In the late '60s, there was distance between us: my hours of piano practice every day, the metronome swinging in lonely arcs, Iver's time on church boards, the late-night clash of TV with piano scales. Then came my long illness of over two years.

My mind landed me for a moment in 1978. I had just been released from the hospital, and I had a feeling of renaissance, of beginning anew. Iver and I had become very close during that time and he had given me a new bright blue Toyota to celebrate my recovery and my ability to drive again. I drove it proudly.

One day a boyfriend and I had a quarrel. A few hours after he had left, I went out to drive my new Toyota, still very upset. Clouds had gathered in a dark purple wound in the north. I was fascinated by the sky, and had always loved summer storms in Iowa. I began to drive straight north toward the storm. Wild flowers grew in clusters along the rough narrow highway. I hummed to the radio.

Then the rain started. It hit the car like bullets. The lightning was like a dazzling sword striking the pavement ahead, and thunder claps sent my heart pounding in rhythm with the rain. Then hail stones began to bounce off the windshield like ping-pong balls. Suddenly, the road ahead was flooded with a threatening river. Water crept into my car. *I must turn around*, I thought. Before I knew it, my car was swept into a ditch on its side like a frightened lame horse, water madly gushing into it. I managed to get out just in time.

Some people were kind enough to pick me up on the road and they took me to their home nearby. After drying off, I called Iver and he came up from Des Moines right away. He didn't say anything, except that he was glad I wasn't hurt. He arranged to have my car towed, took care of my insurance to pay for the damages. Some time later, when my father drove my repaired car back home from the shop, I said, "Iver, that was so awful!" "Well, maybe you learned a lesson from it," he replied. "Maybe you can help *me* some day."

I never forgot that.

A few years later I moved from Iowa to Baltimore to further my musical career. I frequently went home for visits, and one such occasion was a hot, humid summer day. Iver had just hosed down the flower beds. We sat in the living room drinking ice tea, the afternoon humming with birds and insects, and he told me how something had struck him in the back of the neck one night, something powerful, like a fish thrashing on a boat dock.

In later years Iver seemed to recover, coming home from work, patting the sides of his easy chair. I made the piano sing. Branches by the window were ancient hands applauding.

Some time later we found out what was weighing down Iver, a dreaded, ugly illness—Alzheimer's. He became bedridden in a dingy nursing-home room in Des Moines where he and my mother resided. Often, when I visited them, I would give a piano recital, sitting at the piano, my stomach pumping butterflies. The clock wound into the past to the strains of "Clair de Lune" and "Liebestraum." The music's magic sent the people applauding, but I would always run down the hall to Iver's room, knowing that an awful disease kept him away.

Iver would be in his room, his eyes shut like seashells. Mother once said that at night he applauded in his sleep, remembering my piano recitals. In the day, the sun set afire through the window Iver's white nest of hair. Sometimes he asked for a ride in his wheelchair— *his* new car—and I wheeled him up and down the drab halls, he raising his arm, yelling, "Faster, faster, faster! . . ."

I was still crying in our old house, but my mind kept racing through the years. Back in the early '60s, we had an apartment along the shore in Laguna Beach, California. Iver and I were swimming in the ocean one summer day when I was on vacation from college. A huge dark, murky wave rolled over my head. After it had broken, pounding like a hammer on the shore, I found I could no longer touch bottom with my toes. The current began to pull me under, surrounding me like a dark veil. Then I felt Iver's arm around me, holding me up, coughing and choking, holding me up to the sky.

We walked back to our apartment, our feet making maps in the sand. At that age, forgetting how to swim was totally embarrassing to me. I made Iver promise he would never tell anyone what had happened, and he never did.

My mind drifted again. I remembered that time at dusk, 1970, when I had just finished giving a piano lesson. I stood at the top of the steps leading to the back porch. Iver sat in his chair, dozing off. His newspaper had dropped with the last cry of a black bird. I longed to tell him something, to sit across the table from him over a cup of coffee, the clock ticking through an early summer evening. I stared at him, wanting to shake his shoulder like rain from a tree.

But the possibility of sharing conversation was long gone, and now, with Iver gone too, I had only my grief. Alone in the house, still crying rivers, Iver was talking to me, comforting me, dusk reigning from his white hair. The setting sun cast memories on the papered walls. He was telling me not to grieve for him, not to cry, but to play the piano once more.

I remembered when I played "Amazing Grace" for Iver in the nursing home, how he had held out his hand to me, a dreaming look in his eyes. This could be the beginning of a piece in memory of Iver. I sat down at the piano and began to play.

Why Can't They Teach Others What They Know?

D E B O R A H   C A R R O L L

THOSE WERE THE MOST profound words my father
ever spoke to me. They were also his last. A few hours later he was
dead. The irony still makes me smile. I had spent most of his last few
weeks, if not most of my life, trying to get my father to verbalize
some heartfelt thought or feeling. I envisioned us experiencing
poignant father-daughter bonding while we shared the final days of
his life. He would say meaningful things and I would say equally
meaningful things, we would hug and express feelings never before
shared. Unfortunately, by the time he uttered that last question, it was
too late for me to respond.

My father's reluctance to bare his soul should have come as no
surprise to me because he had always been what people refer to as a
man of few words. My friends in high school used to say that if my
dad grunted in their direction, that meant he liked them.

Conversation was never his strong suit, but somehow he let you know how he felt. Or at least you could make a good guess. My father was not an analytical person. He didn't dwell on the reasons behind things; he just accepted what was and dealt with it. Basically, he lived his life without ever asking, "why?"

That philosophy of life without questioning might explain how he managed to get so sick without noticing that something was wrong. My father had lung cancer and it wasn't until his lung collapsed and filled with fluid that he finally saw a doctor. He even mowed his lawn the same week he was diagnosed. At one Friday night dinner, I noticed that his breathing was labored and I urged him to see a doctor the next day. He was admitted to the hospital immediately. The prognosis was grave and I was not sure how much more time I would have with him. I wasn't about to waste a minute. As soon as the doctor left the room, I began telling my father how I felt about him and his impact on my life and the person I am. I had lived thirty-eight years without expressing these feelings and I didn't want him to die without knowing all. His life had made a differ-ence—he was leaving a legacy of love and I knew that no one had told him that before.

My father was not comfortable with warm fuzzy conversation, but there I sat in the hospital room holding nothing back. After my volcano of emotion erupted, he looked at me and poignantly said, "Do you have a key to my safe deposit box?" I took that as a clue that he did not wish me to pursue my monologue about his attributes. We moved on to the business at hand—his death and how it would be handled.

We decided that he would move in with me, my husband and three young daughters. My sister lived in New York and was unable to care for him. He also was not as comfortable with her family because he had not spent as much time with them as he had with us. He wanted to die in my house where he felt at home, and not in a hospital or other unfamiliar place. We didn't know how long it would be but we both readied ourselves in our own ways.

I prepared myself as I usually do for new experiences. I went to the library and read books on caring for the dying. My dad, on the other hand, readied himself in his usual way. He kept on going steadfastly and quietly until he just stopped. The amazing thing was, both of these methods worked. I had read in one of the books that when a person is close to death it helps if you say to her/him, "It's okay to let go." I couldn't picture myself saying that, but then, at the time, I couldn't imagine watching my father die in my den, either. Anyway, I tucked that line into the back of my mind in case the opportunity arose to use it.

The weeks passed slowly. My father was up and around, not bedridden, but I stayed home from work and kept him company. I tried to cook him meals he liked but his appetite seemed to have disappeared. For some reason, he wouldn't come into the kitchen, but calling instructions from the living room, he taught me how to make stuffed cabbage. I wondered why he would not come into the kitchen to be with me while I cooked. The only reason I could think of was that it was too painful to be that close to his normal life without really participating. He passed the time quietly. He taught my daughters card games and we watched TV and movies together. If it hadn't been such a depressing time, it might have been fun. I was sorry I hadn't convinced him long ago to move in with us.

A hospice nurse visited our home to make preparations for her regular visits. She would help my father with his personal hygiene and counsel us on how to live with the dying. She told us that she believed he had about two weeks left to live. I was sort of shocked because he didn't seem so sick. That night, my husband and I explained the situation to our daughters. We let them know that Grandpop was going to die in the house very soon. I said that it wouldn't be that day or even the next, but it would happen soon.

The next day, on what would turn out to be the last day of his life, my father was groggy and semi-delusional. He asked me to wash his hair and discussed the movie "Avalon" with my aunt, his sister. Then he went to sleep. When he woke he said something about his factory having to move from New York to Philadelphia and that he was worried about it. I assured him everything would work out all right, knowing that the factory had made that move successfully in 1962. He woke again, just long enough to ask, "Why can't they teach others what they know?" I wondered briefly if he was speaking to me, or perhaps to spirits of those before him who had come to escort him to the other side. I put such surreal thoughts aside and answered, "I don't know, Dad, but you always taught me." I don't think he heard me, though; he seemed to be asleep.

Throughout the night he kept sitting up and falling over, so my husband and I took turns staying in his room, helping him back to bed over and over again. He seemed so restless and unhappy, it broke my heart to watch him suffer. I wanted to do or say something to help him. So I said the only thing that came into my head. "*Let go, Dad; it's okay to let go.*"

I left his room for a few minutes and when I came back he was peaceful and calm. I was relieved that he seemed so comfortable after so much struggling to breathe. Then I realized that this serenity was death. I was not surprised that he had managed to wait until I left the room to die. I knew that he would have worried about how I would react at that precise moment and he chose to spare me any unnecessary unpleasantness. I hugged him and said good-bye. And I didn't feel sad because I knew he was better off. His ceasing to live just seemed like the natural next step to his life. It felt like a beautiful thing.

My father's last words about teaching were particularly moving in light of the eulogy I had written a few weeks earlier in preparation for his funeral. I wanted to tell people what I knew about my dad that they probably did not know. I wanted his funeral to be warm and loving, as he was. I wrote about what a good teacher he had been even though he had never finished high school. I wrote about how I learned a great deal from my father's example. Most important of all he taught me about parenting through love, patience, and acceptance of people as they are. He also taught me about the importance of forgiveness and generosity.

My father had lived a simple life. He worked in a factory. He loved his wife and children. He didn't ask for much more than he already had. I never heard him complain about how life had been unfair. He seemed content to put in a hard day's work and come home to his family. For most of my life I didn't appreciate his simple ways. He didn't talk much and that made it hard for me to relate to him. I am a verbal person and I need the give and take that conversation affords. We weren't close but we didn't fight either. We just existed without questioning each other's lives. But there was always trust between us even when it was unspoken.

Then my mother died and everything changed. My father was suddenly living alone and I felt obligated to visit him every Friday night. The man who had never so much as boiled water learned how to bake chicken and immediately took up where my mother had left off. When my children were born, these traditional Friday night dinners at Grandpop's became a sweetly anticipated weekly event.

My father was the only babysitter my children ever had and I know that made him as happy as it did them. He didn't change their diapers but he let them eat whatever they wanted and when they were old enough to watch TV, he let them stay up to watch what they pleased. He loved my daughters unconditionally. I think that he was close with them because of the role he played in their lives. He wasn't just a visitor; he was a consistent nurturer and fostered a unique bond between them. If he had just played with them, they surely would have loved him; but because he took care of them, they grew to need and appreciate him in a more substantive way. They still talk about him constantly and usually they express how much they miss him.

Watching the relationship grow between my father and my daughters, I learned a great deal about what children need from the adults in their lives. His grandparenting taught me how to be a better parent. More importantly, I appreciated what a wonderful friend he had become for me as an adult. I could talk to my father about anything and he would listen without judging. He supported any moves I made and always accepted my decisions. He took to my husband as if he were his own son and treated him with the same respect. I grew to love and appreciate him differently than before. I truly liked the person he was and I knew he felt the same way about me. Our relationship had evolved into one of love and respect, not obligation.

I don't regret that we didn't have more time together. I feel lucky to have had him as a friend for as long as I did. I believe that if I had not had children and had not gotten to know the nurturing side of him, we would have never developed the closeness that we had during the last ten years. I've thought a lot about mothers and daughters and the closeness that can develop between them. I feel fortunate to have experienced that bond with my father.

Sometimes I felt guilty about taking so much and giving so little in return, but I hope my father would have said that I did give something back to him. When he became ill, I felt that at last I could return some of the care he had given me and my family for so many years. People kept telling me what a wonderful thing I was doing taking care of him. They didn't understand that it was Sid who was doing the wonderful thing. He was *letting* me take care of him.

The day my father died I felt his presence all around me, and now, more than a year later, I still do. He taught me how to live and I told him that. What I didn't get a chance to say is that he also taught me how to die. I no longer fear death after witnessing the peace it brought him. I had asked him if he felt scared about dying and he said there was nothing to be afraid of. I think he was right.

I plan to live the rest of my life teaching my children all that their grandfather taught me. Maybe I won't wait until my time is up to pass on his final message. "Teach others what you know."

TO MAKE HIM PROUD

GLORIA AVERBUCH

ON THAT SUMMER AFTERNOON when my step-brother called to tell me my father had suddenly died—for no apparent reason but that it was "his time"—it was not just that the world seemed to stand still. Worse, it was as if it exploded on the spot.

As I sat staring blankly at the lines on my wooden kitchen table, the phone cord negligently tangled around the stove, I felt my body jump out of its skin, as if I could instantly escape being me. I heard my own voice repeatedly shout the inevitable, "Oh no!" It was a voice I did not recognize, an animal sound. I can still remember myself when I look at that room. That sound still echoes from the walls.

It wasn't supposed to be. Certainly not now—and to the naïve little girl I still was at age 40—not ever. He was an extremely vital, young-looking age 72, who, like me, ran every day for physical and mental fitness. He worked full-time—a well-known city leader in San Francisco, a city he loved, and to which he devoted the considerable energy of his upbeat, vibrant spirit. But quietly, unexpectedly, and at the same age and in the same manner as his own father, he fell asleep on June 2, 1991, for the last time.

For me, hearing this news has a universal comparison: the day President Kennedy was assassinated. They say if you were of any conscious age, you still recall exactly where you were, and what you were doing when you heard the news. You remember how you felt, or rather, how you stopped feeling, for that moment in time.

My father was my JFK. He was my hero, my leader. And like so many heroes, he seemed immortal. Yes, these men had their faults, but that's not what I recall. Like the President who charmed and guided a nation, my father was my rock, my inspiration. He was also largely the reason I had survived emotionally after my mother left when I was eight years old. Inadvertently, to a large degree my life became modeled on his. He worked in journalism and public relations. I have too. He wrote books, so do I. He was an avid athlete. So am I.

Streams of people approached me at his memorial service, or wrote me, to tell me what I have always known: Bernie Averbuch was a rare and extraordinary man. As a father, he was revolutionary for his time. In the late 1950s, he was forced to persuade an unwilling judge to give him custody of his children, despite the fact that my mother agreed to the plan. He faced a world filled with prejudice about his ability as a man to raise children, and he undertook the task amid the often-expressed skepticism of relatives and peers. Needless to say, this was not the era of support for the involved father. But this man—in his early 30s, completely on his own and with limited financial resources—took responsibility for a six-year-old son and an eight-year-old daughter. Several years ago he told me that not only had it never occurred to him to do otherwise, but that his memories of raising us were joyful. (You have to be a parent—and to know the kind of adolescent I was—to soak in that one!)

My father never remarried, although after my brother and I were grown he met a woman with whom he shared this life for the last 17 years. "I met a nice Jewish girl," he wrote me, much like the shy, young man he surely once was. I am particularly close to Adrienne— a part of my father that lives on—as are my children, who know her as Grandma.

As my father encouraged and allowed me to bloom in rare form, so too did he with others. Adrienne talks about the emergence of her selfhood during her life with my father—this reminds me of my own self. Adrienne is legally both her first and last name. It was while knowing my father that my stepmother decided that she need not retain the name of either her ex-husband or her absent father.

My father was a feminist before the word defined a social movement. He raised me to be an adventurer, and to be strong: both literally and figuratively. He was an accomplished tennis player and teacher of the sport, and with encouragement and tutelage, he nurtured my own athletic skills. Tennis, ice skating, ballet, swimming, hiking—I learned to use my body like some learn foreign languages.

Together with my brother, our family bonding was seasonal: baseball in summer, football in fall, and basketball in winter. These "games" became more than just a memory of my childhood; they became a metaphor for my life. What's more, sports has stayed with me as an adult and a parent, both as an avocation and a vocation.

My father believed in teaching me the ability to face life without fear, and he did so literally. When I was six years old, he pointed to the top of the playground monkey bars and said, "Why don't you do a handstand." Initially, I was appalled. It was so high, my feet would touch the clouds, I protested. "I'll help you," he wisely added. I will never forget how far the ground below looked from my dizzy vision. Nor will I ever forget going back to those monkey bars years later, when with a smile of understanding and gratitude, I reached up and easily touched the top of those bars.

The ability to grow up, and to move on, was a gift my father gave me. He tirelessly lobbied for me to go out into the world, much in the way he had done, leaving his native Chicago in his early 20s to settle in California. At first, and for a long time, I resisted him. I was young; I was terrified to leave the security of what I knew. But that day did come when I instinctively got the message, heard the call. From the moment I strapped on a backpack—that classic symbol of a young student in the 1970's—I literally fell in love with traveling. In travel, I felt not only the thrill of freedom and possibility, but I conquered the adolescent pain that had so long crippled me. By my mid-20s, I had touched down in 30 countries. Among them was Israel, a place where I lived for three years, and which has become a second home.

But perhaps the most difficult trip I ever took was a permanent one. In 1979, experiencing the excruciating pain that follows the breakup of a serious relationship, I spent three weeks in New York City contemplating my next move. I decided to return home to San Francisco, where I sat on the back steps of the house where I had grown up looking into my father's eyes with a childhood plea that said, "Take care of me." Gazing down to shed my private tears, I picked at the perpetually chipped gray paint of those steps. I listened to my father soothe me, but again, as he always had done, he encouraged me to swim in deep water. "You can stay if you decide to, but I encourage you to go back to New York and make it there." So I moved from a small town in Oregon to Manhattan—3,000 literal miles and a million figurative ones from everything I knew—a place where I had no job and no family. It remains one of the hardest things I have ever done. Yet from the moment I arrived, I knew in my heart it was the best thing I ever could have done.

My father's encouragement to explore and take new roads enabled me to marry at the age of 32. I married according to the custom and the values which had been nurtured by him. Partly in my father's honor, I kept my name. My husband Paul (who is seven years younger than I) and I were wed by a woman rabbi, who placed not just the one traditional glass for the man, but two glasses for each of our feet to crush. The symbol, the journey, the destiny was meant to belong to us both. After our vows, it is the embrace of my father with my husband which I will always recall. For as long as they knew one another, those two men loved and admired each other.

Photos of my father still reawaken the pain of his absence. There's a series of photos on my wall I gaze upon when I have the courage. The one in the middle shows my father holding me as a baby. On either side is one of each of my daughters at the same age, in the same spot in Golden Gate Park in San Francisco. My husband, dressed in a similar jacket and loafers as my father, sits with the girls in the same pose as my father. I shudder at the resemblance of these two men, which I had never noticed before. "You don't have to be a shrink to figure out this one!" I often say to my friends with a laugh. Of all the men I have known, I must surely have recognized that the goodness of my father resides in the soul of the one I married.

In 1986, before my first child was born, my husband and I decided that we would divide our work week and childcare (which remains our arrangement six years later). With a parent as involved as my own father had been, how could I have done otherwise? Paul also asked me if I would like to give our children my last name. It was in honor of my father. "From generation to generation, we shall remember your name." I recited that Hebrew phrase at his funeral. Now, whenever I hear my daughters' names, Yael and Shira Averbuch, I feel not only the sting of my father's absence, but a gladness for that part of him that remains.

Increasingly, I am in awe of my father's parenting. I see his gifts so clearly now, particularly when I face the decisions and the daily mixture of conflict and emotion that all parents inevitably do. I strive to do it right, like he did. Few parents raise their children with the combination of strength, confidence, and natural ability my father possessed. Few can love and *truly* let go. Only now—as I struggle with the instinct to cling to my children even more in my father's absence—do I fully realize how strong, and how exceptional, he was. In times of infinite personal trials, he managed, as a parent, to display an almost zen-like grace.

As a parent, it could not have been easy for him to let me take roads that were clearly the wrong ones, and to remain silent. "You must let them fall in order that they can learn to get up," I tell myself today in recognition of that skill. I remember when I was one semester away from obtaining my college degree, I sat across from my father at a restaurant table and told him I was thinking of dropping out of school—yet again—to travel to South America. (I had just returned from Mexico—a trip he had to know was loaded with danger and risks). A parent now myself, I know I could never have reacted as he did. I imagine that my knuckles would turn white from squeezing the table legs in a supreme effort to remain calm. Yet there was no such sign of tension as he said in reply, "Do what you have to do."

One year after my father's death, I relived the pain and pride I felt at his funeral and memorial service. On an appropriately sunny day in San Francisco, the city he helped make beautiful, a memorial to him was unveiled in the center of downtown. On it is a plaque with the words I composed: "Bernard Averbuch, 1919-1991, The Mayor of Market Street. He gave his love and talents to this City." The Mayor spoke, others spoke, somehow even I spoke. Despite the wonder and beauty of the day, the pain invaded me anew, a pain that continues to reverberate in all that I feel and do.

One year after his death, I look down into a black hole and into that pain. It is a hole that even a wonderful husband, healthy children, and a good career cannot fill. I know now that they were not meant to. Many mornings I wake from yet another of those dreams—"You've made a mistake" I say to all those who would have me believe he has died. "Here he is!" I call out as my father walks toward me, his face bright with sunlight. I sit with my morning coffee and remind myself that I must learn to mourn, and yet I must move on. How hard that is without that person who had always helped me go forward!

This essay isn't about peace of soul or mind, about feeling and knowing my father's spirit still lives (although I know with absolute clarity that it does). This is about grief and anger and pain—loud and raucous. It's about an admiration, an identity, so wound around my father, that I cannot fathom how to put it in its proper place, or even know if there is one. It's not only about the failure to gracefully accept his death, but the shame I feel at my inability to appreciate what I had with the man, who lived a relatively long and happy life.

Since his death, I realize my father has not stopped gently pushing me out into the world, just as he did since the day I could first walk. But this is a big push—into a world where I must truly stand alone. I must confront the most obvious and absolute of truths—that of death—his, my own, and everyone's. Ironically, my father died just two months after my 40th birthday. As we raised our glasses in a toast, I looked around the table of friends and family and felt the joy and wholeness tinged by an eerie premonition that it could not last. Even then I had an unsettling sense that this age, this time, would be a landmark in my life. Little did I understand its impact. "There's no free lunch," I often sarcastically remark on reflection of that evening.

As I write this, I can hear the laughter of my children outside. And just as I enter the black hole, I know in my head—if not yet in my heart—that I must climb out of it, absorb the anger and grief, and move past them. I must arrive at a place of some reconciliation. After all, that is what my father would want. And making him proud is what I want. I always have. After all, he was my Dad.

BIOGRAPHICAL NOTES

SHIRLEY ABBOTT, who was born and raised in Hot Springs, Arkansas, currently lives in New York. She works in Manhattan as a writer for a health newsletter and has also written a previous book, *Womenfolks: Growing Up Down South* (Ticknor and Fields, 1991).

GLORIA AVERBUCH is the author of three books on running and fitness. She is currently working on a book with Olympic gold medalist Joan Samuelson. Averbuch can also be heard on WABC and WFAN radio in New York.

JULIA BANKS grew up on the northern shore of Lake Michigan. She studied English Literature at Western Michigan University, and is now an editor with a publishing company in Connecticut.

AMY BIANCOLLI, an arts and entertainment reporter for the Albany *Times Union*, is writing a biography of violin virtuoso Fritz Kreisler. She received her B.A. from Hamilton College and her M.A. from

Columbia University Graduate School of Journalism. She lives in Albany with her husband, journalist Christopher Ringwald, and daughter, Madeleine Margaret.

ANTOINETTE BOSCO has been Executive Editor of *The Litchfield County Times* since 1982. She has written more than 200 magazine articles as well as five books, and is currently at work on a book about how pain alters our lives—for better or worse—titled *The Pummeled Heart* (Twenty-third Publications, 1994).

JANET BURROWAY was raised in Phoenix, Arizona, and attended Barnard College, Cambridge University, England, and the Yale School of Drama. She is the author of plays, poetry, children's books, and seven novels including *The Buzzards, Raw Silk, Opening Nights*, and *Cutting Stone*. Her most recent work is a full-length play, *Medea with Child*. Her textbook *Writing Fiction* (HarperCollege, 1991), in its third edition, is used in more than three hundred colleges and universities in the U.S. She is the McKenzie Professor of Literature and Writing at the Florida State University in Tallahassee.

BEBE MOORE CAMPBELL has been an award winner of the National Endowment for the Arts Literature Grant, the National Association of Negro Business and Professional Women's Literature Award, and the Midwestern Radio Theater Workshop Competition. Her books include *Successful Women, Angry Men: Backlash in the Two-Career Marriage,* and *Your Blues Ain't Like Mine* (Putnam, 1992), a novel.

DEBORAH CARROLL is the Newspaper in Education Manager for *The Philadelphia Inquirer* and *Daily News*. She is the author of the book *Good News,* (Penguin USA). She lives in Elkins Park, Pennsylvania, with her husband and three daughters.

ANDREA CHAPIN received her M.F.A. in creative writing from
Columbia University. She has worked in Mexico, studied in Spain,
and acted professionally in Germany. She is the editor of *The New
Theater Review* and an associate editor of the literary journal
Conjunctions. She lives in New York City and is currently completing
her first novel.

MELISSA DRIBBEN is a graduate of Tufts University and holds a
master's degree in international affairs from Columbia University.
Deciding against a diplomatic career, she became a reporter for the
San Antonio Light and the *San Antonio Express-News* in Texas, and
then for *The Bergen Record* in New Jersey. She has also written for UPI
and *Newsday*, and currently serves as metro columnist at *The Philadelphia Inquirer*. She lives in Pennsylvania with her husband and
three children.

ELAINE ERICKSON is a composer, pianist, and writer. Her poems
have been published in numerous poetry journals, and she has pre-
sented her music compositions in concerts throughout the country.
She has won three awards from the *Lyrical Iowa* poetry journal, and
three volumes of her work have been published by Chestnut Hills
Press. She lives in Baltimore, Maryland, with her cat Flora.

MARCIA FALK, an Affiliated Scholar at Stanford University's
Institute for Research on Women and Gender, is the author of two
books of poems, *It Is July in Virginia* (Rara Avis, 1985) and *This
Year in Jerusalem* (State Street Press, 1986). Her books of translation
include *The Song of Songs: A New Translation and Interpretation*
(HarperSan Francisco, 1990) and *With Teeth in the Earth:
Selected Poems of Malka Heifetz Tussman* (Wayne State University
Press, 1992). She is currently writing *The Book of Blessings: A*

Feminist-Jewish Reconstruction of Prayer (HarperSan Francisco, 1994).

MORGAN HENDERSON, an applied psychologist, now writes fiction full-time in Lansdowne, Pennsylvania. A pioneer in the field of death and dying, from 1978 to 1982 she traveled throughout the U.S. and Canada to provide counseling, training, and support for professionals, patients, and family members coping with grief and loss. She is co-author, with E. Paul Torrance, et. al., of *Save Tomorrow for the Children* (Beasly Ltd., 1987), a worldwide study of creativity in children.

SOPHIA LOREN is an internationally renowned Italian-born actress whose career spans more than forty years.

DEA ADRIA MALLIN is Associate Professor of English at Community College of Philadelphia. Her articles have appeared in the *Washington Post, The Philadelphia Inquirer, The Boston Globe,* and such national publications as *Islands, Woman's Own,* and various airline magazines. She has also been a co-anchor at WPVI-TV in Philadelphia. In her free time, Dea enjoys swimming, bicycling, and hiking, and volunteers on scientific expeditions with Earthwatch.

MARY MARTIN NIEPOLD is a freelance writer for *The New York Times,* Associated Press, and various magazines. Her syndicated fashion column with Newspaper Enterprise Association is distributed throughout the U.S., Latin America, and Europe. Before moving to New York, she was a features writer with *The Philadelphia Inquirer* for 14 years. She grew up in Lexington, N.C., and holds a B.A. in English and Theology from Wake Forest University.

CHRISTINE O'HAGAN worked as a telephone operator, stock transfer clerk, bank teller, and researcher for the CBS television network, though she knew that she wanted to be a writer. Her first article, "Serendipity Son," was published in *The New York Times* in 1982, and won first prize in the Jerry Lewis Writing Awards Contest. She served an internship at The Feminist Press and attended the Summer Writer's Conference at Southampton University in 1987. Her first novel, *Benediction at the Savoia* (Harcourt Brace Jovanovich, 1992), received laudatory reviews. She is currently at work on a second novel.

KIM RICH is a contributing writer for *The Anchorage Daily News*. The author of *Johnny's Girl: A Daughter's Memoir of Growing Up in Alaska's Underworld* (William Morrow & Company, 1993), she is a candidate for the M.F.A. in Creative Writing at Columbia University.

NANCY BAKER RULLO, teacher, poet, student, actor, gardener, mother of Tara and Maeve, life partner of Tony, daughter of the late Jack Baker and Flo Baker, is pleased that *June 24, 1952* will be her first published essay. It is one of a series recreating her life in the 1940s and 1950s.

CONSTANCE SCHRAFT was born in New Rochelle, New York. Her work has appeared in *The New Yorker*, and she has written the novel *Instead of You* (Ticknor and Fields, 1990). She lives in New York City with her husband and two sons.

DOLORES SCHWARTZ is an Assistant Professor of English at a southern university. She is married and has two grown children. A feminist activist, Schwartz has published numerous articles and is currently at work on a biography.

JOAN ALLISON SHIEL grew up on Long Island and has lived in New York City for more than 35 years. She is currently involved in various history and preservation projects after a long career in sales and marketing. She is a graduate of Pace University.

KAREN STABINER is a contributing editor for the *Los Angeles Times Magazine*, and she writes about west coast advertising for *The New York Times*. Her articles appear in many national magazines, and she has written three books: *Limited Engagements*, a novel; *Courting Fame*, about amateur tennis players; and *Inventing Desire: Inside Chiat-Day: The Hottest Shops, The Coolest Players, The Big Business of Advertising*.

CANDYCE H. STAPEN specializes in writing about family and psychological issues, and travel. She is a contributing editor at *Vacations* magazine and writes columns for *Family Travel Times*, and is a columnist for the *Washington Times* and *USA Weekend*. Her articles appear in numerous magazines and newspapers, and she has written several books, including *Fifty Great Family Vacations: Eastern North America* and *Fifty Great Family Vacations: Western North America* (Globe Pequot). Her *Blue Guide to Washington, D.C.* (Norton and Black) will soon be available in bookstores.

STEPHANIE S. TOLAN is a popular writer of fiction for children and young adults. Her books include *Marcy Hooper and the Greatest Treasure in the World, Plague Year,* and *A Good Courage*, chosen as Best Book of the Year by *School Library Journal*. Tolan has also written several articles on the subject of gifted children, as well as a book on the topic, called *Guiding the Gifted Child*.

THE CHARITIES

Proceeds from this book will benefit the following charities:

The AMERICAN HEART ASSOCIATION (AHA), founded in 1924, is the oldest and largest national non-profit voluntary health association dedicated to reducing disability and death from cardiovascular diseases and stroke. Each year, more than 3.6 million volunteers help the AHA fight cardiovascular diseases by means of research, professional and public education, and community service. For further information, contact: American Heart Association National Center, 7272 Greenville Avenue, Dallas, TX 75231–4596. Telephone: (214) 373–6300 or 1–800–AHA–USA1.

The CHILDREN'S CRISIS TREATMENT CENTER (CCTC) is a private, non-profit, community-supported mental health and child development facility that provides social and therapeutic services for traumatized children and their families. CCTC specializes in treating young children who have been the victims of sexual and physical abuse, severe neglect, or who have witnessed traumatic acts of violence. CCTC provides social work services including comprehensive family assessment, education, and individual therapy and counseling. For further information, contact: Children's Crisis Treatment Center, 1823 Callowhill Street, Philadelphia, PA 19130–4197. Telephone: (215) 496–0742.

READING IS FUNDAMENTAL (RIF), America's largest and oldest children's literacy organization, serves 3 million young people each year through a grassroots network staffed by more than 150,000 volunteers. RIF, a nonprofit organization, develops projects that focus community and family attention on the importance of reading. Reaching into schools, libraries, hospitals, homeless shelters, and other targeted areas, RIF seeks to motivate children with the message that "Reading is fun!" For further information, contact: Reading Is Fundamental, Inc., 600 Maryland Avenue, S. W., Suite 600, Washington, D.C. 20024. Telephone: (202) 287–3371.